Life During the Middle Ages

Titles in The Way People Live series include:

THE WAY
PEOPLE
LIVE

Life During the Middle Ages

by Earle Rice Jr.

Lucent Books, P.O. Box 289011, San Diego, CA 92198-9011

Library of Congress Cataloging-in-Publication Data

Rice, Earle.
    Life during the Middle Ages / by Earle Rice, Jr.
       p.   cm. — (The way people live)
    Includes bibliographical references and index.
    Summary: Describes country and city life during the Middle Ages includ-
ing such aspects as social order, religion, family life, agriculture, money and
trade, war, pestilence, education, and architecture and other arts.
    ISBN 1-56006-386-6 (lib. bdg. : alk. paper)
    1. Civilization, Medieval—Juvenile literature.   [1. Civilization,
Medieval.] I. Title. II. Series.
CB351.R47   1998
909.07—dc21
                                                    97-48275
                                                       CIP
                                                       AC

Printed in the U.S.A.

Contents

Discovering the Humanity in Us All

The Way People Live series focuses on pockets of human culture. Some of these are current cultures, like the Eskimos of the Arctic; others no longer exist, such as the Jewish ghetto in Warsaw during World War II. What many of these cultural pockets share, however, is the fact that they have been viewed before, but not completely understood.

To really understand any culture, it is necessary to strip the mind of the common notions we hold about groups of people. These stereotypes are the archenemies of learning. It does not even matter whether the stereotypes are positive or negative; they are confining and tight. Removing them is a challenge that's not easily met, as anyone who has ever tried it will admit. Ideas that do not fit into the templates we create are unwelcome visitors—ones we would prefer remain quietly in a corner or forgotten room.

The cowboy of the Old West is a good example of such confining roles. The cowboy was courageous, yet soft-spoken. His time (it is always a he, in our template) was spent alternatively saving a rancher's daughter from certain death on a runaway stagecoach, or shooting it out with rustlers. At times, of course, he was likely to get a little crazy in town after a trail drive, but for the most part, he was the epitome of inner strength. It is disconcerting to find out that the cowboy is human, even a bit childish. Can it really be true that cowboys would line up to help the cook on the trail drive grind coffee, just hoping he would give them a little stick of pep-

permint candy that came with the coffee shipment? The idea of tough cowboys vying with one another to help "Coosie" (as they called their cooks) for a bit of candy seems silly and out of place.

So is the vision of Eskimos playing video games and watching MTV, living in prefab housing in the Arctic. It just does not fit with what "Eskimo" means. We are far more comfortable with snow igloos and whale blubber, harpoons and kayaks.

Although the cultures dealt with in Lucent's The Way People Live series are often historically and socially well known, the emphasis is on the personal aspects of life. Groups of people, while unquestionably affected by their politics and their governmental structures, are more than those institutions. How do people in a particular time and place educate their children? What do they eat? And how do they build their houses? What kinds of work do they do? What kinds of games do they enjoy? The answers to these questions bring these cultures to life. People's lives are revealed in the particulars and only by knowing the particulars can we understand these cultures' will to survive and their moments of weakness and greatness.

This is not to say that understanding politics does not help to understand a culture. There is no question that the Warsaw ghetto, for example, was a culture that was brought about by the politics and social ideas of Adolf Hitler and the Third Reich. But the Jews who were crowded together in the ghetto cannot be understood by the Reich's politics. Their life was a day-to-day battle for existence, and the creativity and methods they used to prolong their lives is a vital story of human perseverance that would be denied by focusing only on the institutions of Hitler's Germany. Knowing that children as young as five or six outwitted Nazi guards on a daily basis, that Jewish policemen helped the Germans control the ghetto, that children attended secret schools in the ghetto and even earned diplomas—these are the things that reveal the fabric of life, that can inspire, intrigue, and amaze.

Books in The Way People Live series allow both the casual reader and the student to see humans as victims, heroes, and onlookers. And although humans act in ways that can fill us with feelings of sorrow and revulsion, it is important to remember that "hero," "predator," and "victim" are dangerous terms. Heaping undue pity or praise on people reduces them to objects, and strips them of their humanity.

Seeing the Jews of Warsaw only as victims is to deny their humanity. Seeing them only as they appear in surviving photos, staring at the camera with infinite sadness, is limiting, both to them and to those who want to understand them. To an object of pity, the only appropriate response becomes "Those poor creatures!" and that reduces both the quality of their struggle and the depth of their despair. No one is served by such two-dimensional views of people and their cultures.

With this in mind, The Way People Live series strives to flesh out the traditional, two-dimensional views of people in various cultures and historical circumstances. Using a wide variety of primary quotations—the words not only of the politicians and government leaders, but of the real people whose lives are being examined—each book in the series attempts to show an honest and complete picture of a culture removed from our own by time or space.

By examining cultures in this way, the reader will notice not only the glaring differences from his or her own culture, but also will be struck by the similarities. For indeed, people share common needs—warmth, good company, stability, and affirmation from others. Ultimately, seeing how people really live, or have lived can only enrich our understanding of ourselves.

A Thousand Years of Transition

During the first five centuries A.D., barbarians overran the British Isles and much of the European continent, toppling existing empires and wreaking general havoc in the Western world. Moreover, according to Italian historian Robert S. Lopez, chairman of medieval studies at Yale University since 1946, the triumph of the barbarians

> did not bring in its train a new force of a kind to stimulate healthy reaction. It only accelerated the already pronounced decadence of the exhausted peoples of the empires.

> In the West, the dissolution of the [Roman] Empire in the fifth century brought into being a number of barbarian states of moderate size, carved out haphazardly in the course of conquests or scuffles between neighbors.[1]

By the start of the sixth century A.D., Greece's splendor had long since faded, Rome's glory was of another day, and the fragmented barbarian states wallowed in the throes of decay. A restructuring of Western civilization was not only sorely needed but imminent.

Medieval Periods and Related Terms

The onset of the Middle Ages—considered by most scholars to be the millennium between 500 and 1500—heralded the birth of a new cultural experience in Europe. Many scholars and historians subdivide the Middle Ages into the Early Middle Ages (500 to 900 or 1000), the High Middle Ages (900 or 1000 to about 1300), and the Late Middle Ages (1300 to 1500). Together the three periods formed a thousand-year bridge "between the passing of the classical civilization of the Mediterranean and the coming of Modern European civilization."[2]

Other terms associated with the same time frame often cause confusion and should be used with care. For example, the witty and learned authors Judy Jones and William Wilson write:

> *The Dark Ages* is what Renaissance people, looking down their aquiline noses, called the whole of the Middle Ages. Scholars, however, stepping in once again, preempted the term for [reassigned it to] the Early Middle Ages only, arguing that the five centuries after the year 1000 weren't, give or take the Hundred Years' War, the Crusades, the Spanish Inquisition, and the Great Plague, really as bad as all that.

> *Medieval times*—or the medieval era, or whatever—is simply, and literally, a Latinate way of saying "Middle Ages," from the Latin *medius*, "middle," plus *ævum*, "age." And *feudalism* describes not a period of time but a political system that prevailed during it, in which vassals (the ancestors of our nobles) pledge fealty

(our loyalty) to their liege lord (our king) exchanging their service in time of war for inheritable fiefs (our real estate). As it happens, feudalism was in effect in most of Europe from about the tenth century until the end of the fourteenth. But while it coincides with much of the Middle Ages, that doesn't mean you get to substitute one term for the other.[3]

More specifically, feudalism flourished for only about one-half of the medieval period.

The Heritage of the Ancient World

The transition from the classical age to the Renaissance and Reformation of the 1500s and 1600s did not just happen, of course, it evolved. As Norman F. Cantor, professor of history, sociology, and comparative literature at New York University, observes,

> European medieval civilization was not produced by any one event or series of events, but by the absorption by western Europe of certain ways of life, ideas, and religious attitudes that had prevailed for many centuries in the Mediterranean world. These ideas and values were pulled northward into western Europe—into northern France, southern England, northern Italy, and the Rhine valley—and in the process, certain aspects of Mediterranean culture were adapted and changed. (It is perhaps even more significant that many aspects were not changed.) Before the Middle Ages, then, there was a Mediterranean culture and society that

The Vandals, one of the barbarian tribes that would bring down the Roman Empire, march on Rome. The barbarian tribes made many cultural and political contributions to medieval society.

was adopted and absorbed. An understanding of that civilization is essential to an understanding of the Medieval world.

Cantor points out that an Egyptian king mummified in 2500 B.C. and brought back to life in France in 800 A.D. would not have felt distressed by the social system he found. Continues Cantor:

> In a sense, then, the heritage of the ancient world set the conditions for medieval society. Although it is true that the Middle Ages . . . were a distinct and separate civilization in many respects, still medieval men were not able to create just the world they chose: they had to work with what they inherited. They began with a definite set of social forms, political and economic institutions, and ideas and attitudes.[4]

Cantor asserts, for example, that the social and political forms that came to exist in Egypt and Mesopotamia by 3000 B.C. were handed down through the ages. These sociopolitical forms were passed along—with fewer substantial changes than might be expected—first to the Hellenistic (Greek) empires that arose in the Mediterranean basin between 350 and 100 B.C., then to the Roman Empire, and finally to the medieval world. So it comes as no surprise that the barbarians who toppled the Roman Empire with spear and sword also wielded a heavy hand in shaping the evolving medieval society in western Europe.

The Barbarian Influence

Although the early medieval period is often referred to as the Dark Ages, it was also a time of renewal. Even as surges of barbarian invaders—Goths, Vandals, Lombards, Franks, Angles, Saxons, and many others—ran roughshod over a Roman civilization in decay, they broke new ground for constructing a European community founded on cruder, more robust ideas of their own. The barbarian conquests influenced European evolution in endless ways, notably, economically, ethnically, politically, and historically. Comments historian Will Durant:

> Economically it meant reruralization. The barbarians lived by tillage, herding, hunting, and war, and had not yet learned the commercial complexities on which cities thrived; with their victory the municipal character of Western civilization ceased for seven centuries. Ethnically the migrations brought a new mingling of racial elements—a substantial infusion of Germanic blood into Italy, Gaul, and Spain, and of Asiatic blood into Russia, the Balkans, and Hungary. The mixture did not mystically reinvigorate the Italian or Gallic population.

Instead, according to Durant, the new ethnic mixture created an environment in which weak individuals and racial strains were eliminated through war and other competitive pursuits. This, in turn, compelled the citizenry to develop personal strength, stamina, courage, and other such qualities that city dwellers, accustomed to a more secure, comfortable lifestyle, had allowed to lapse. Continuing, Durant notes:

> Politically the conquest replaced a higher with a lower form of monarchy; it augmented the authority of persons, and reduced the power and protection of laws; individualism and violence increased. Historically, the conquest destroyed the out-

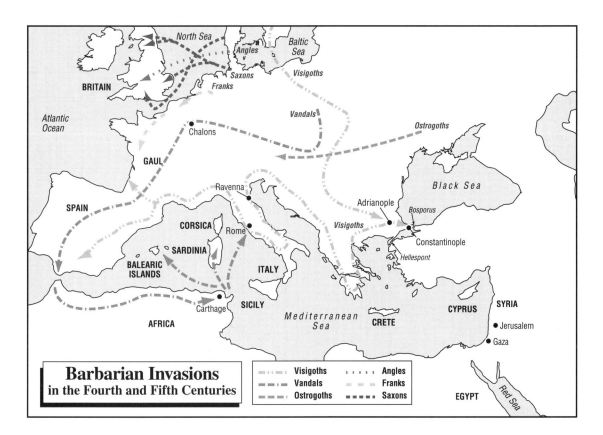

Barbarian Invasions
in the Fourth and Fifth Centuries

Legend:
- ⋅⋅⋅⋅ Visigoths
- ⋅―⋅― Vandals
- ―⋅―⋅ Ostrogoths
- ⋅⋅⋅⋅⋅ Angles
- ⋅⋅⋅⋅ Franks
- ■―■ Saxons

Map labels: North Sea, Baltic Sea, Angles, Visigoths, Saxons, Franks, BRITAIN, Atlantic Ocean, Vandals, Ostrogoths, Chalons, GAUL, Ravenna, Black Sea, SPAIN, Adrianople, Bosporus, CORSICA, Rome, Visigoths, Constantinople, SARDINIA, Hellespont, BALEARIC ISLANDS, ITALY, Carthage, SICILY, Mediterranean Sea, CRETE, CYPRUS, SYRIA, AFRICA, Jerusalem, Gaza, EGYPT, Red Sea

ward form of what had already inwardly decayed; it cleared away with regrettable brutality and thoroughness a system of life which, with all its gifts of order, culture, and law, had worn itself into senile debility, and had lost the powers of regeneration and growth. A new beginning was now possible: the Empire in the West faded, but the states of modern Europe were born.[5]

Another scholar writes of the barbarian influence, "Those ideas that most influenced the development of Europe arose from the barbarian belief in the rights of the individual."[6] Indeed, Europe's "new beginning" drew much of its impetus from a changing attitude toward human rights.

During the Roman Empire, the rights of the state were valued over those of the individual. Romans had subjugated women and imposed an elitist government and legal system on their citizens. Barbarians, in contrast, strongly supported the rights of the individual, which engendered their respect for women and produced their crude but representative system of government and laws. For example, tribal councils elected kings and chiefs and acted as courts of law when necessary.

Battles played an important role in barbarian society. In fact, women often accompanied their tribe into battle and were known to sometimes avert defeat with their rallying cries when the entire tribe faltered. Barbarian leaders led by courageous example. If a leader cringed in the face of an enemy, the tribe immediately hailed another warrior as his replacement.

Leadership, of course, plays a vital role in the success of almost any enterprise, not least the birth of a nation. Courageous leadership and a propensity for the sword enabled barbarian hordes to overrun much of Europe and part of North Africa during the Early Middle Ages. Yet, of all the barbarian factions, only one succeeded in establishing an enduring state: the Franks. The first great Frankish leader after Rome's collapse was Clovis (465–511), who founded the kingdom in Gaul that would later become France.

The Christian Connection

Most barbarians adhered to the principles of Arianism, the dogma of Arius, a third-century Greek theologian. Arius purported that the Son (Christ) is not of the same substance as the Father (God) but was created as an agent for creating the world. The Roman Catholic Church condemned Arianism as heresy. When Clovis converted to Catholicism in 496, the bishop of Rome—that is, the pope—started lending support to Clovis and his Franks.

At this juncture, Christianity began lifting the shroud of darkness that had blanketed Europe during the so-called Dark Ages. The monks of the church, in their isolated monasteries, had managed to preserve the remnants of Roman culture—knowledge of the arts, crafts, and industries. Through missionaries they began to spread this knowledge across the byways of Europe.

Christianity's influence in western Europe continued to broaden over the next two centuries, gaining even further impetus when the great Charlemagne became king of the Franks. Commenting on this legendary monarch, historian James Harpur writes:

> Son of Pepin the Short, Charlemagne, or Charles the Great, the greatest king of

the Franks, came to the throne in 768. For the next 46 years, this bull-necked warrior king applied his energy, determination, and powers of leadership to expanding the Frankish kingdom, converting the heathen, and revitalizing the culture and learning, thus earning himself the sobriquet "the father of Europe."

Charlemagne, notes Harpur, mounted some sixty campaigns during his reign, defeating the Avars in what is now Hungary, fighting the Muslims in Spain, and crushing the Lombards (Langobardi, or "Long Beards") in Italy. Harpur suggests:

> Perhaps his most bitter struggle was against the Saxons in northeastern Germany. For a period of about 30 years, Charlemagne fought these fierce pagans, eventually subduing them and forcibly converting them to Christianity. And he did not shrink from using extreme measures

along the way: after one victory, he slaughtered 4,500 prisoners and deported 10,000 Saxons to the west of the Rhine [River].[7]

During his reign, Charlemagne doubled the size of the Frankish kingdom and converted untold thousands—if not hundreds of thousands—of pagans to Christianity.

In 800, during a Christmas Mass held in St. Peter's in Rome, Pope Leo III rewarded the warrior king's years of service to the church. Placing a crown on Charlemagne's head, the appreciative pope prompted his enthusiastic followers to call out three times: "To Charles Augustus, crowned by God, great and pacific emperor of the Romans, Life and Victory!"[8]

After Charlemagne

When the great Charlemagne died in 814, his kingdom passed to weak descendants, who lacked his vision and determination to preserve and improve a strong union of Franks.

Four Types of Monks

After the collapse of the Roman Empire, monks were instrumental in passing along the residue of Rome's cultural heritage to succeeding generations of Europeans. In Rules for Monks, *St. Benedict of Nursia, a sixth-century Roman aristocrat and monastic leader, categorizes monks into four types. The following extract forms a part of* The Medieval Reader, *edited by Norman F. Cantor.*

"It is evident that there are four types of monks. The first are the Cenobites: that is, those who live in monasteries, serving under a rule and an abbot.

The second type is that of the Anchorites, or Hermits: that is, those who, not in the first fervor of conversion, but after long probation in a monastery, having been taught by the example of many brothers, have learned to fight against the devil and are well prepared to go forth from the ranks of their brothers to solitary combat in the desert. They are now able, with God's assistance, to fight against the vices of the flesh and evil thoughts without the encouragement of a companion, using only their own strength.

The third and worst type of monks is that of the Sarabites, who have not been tested by any rule or the lessons of experience, as gold is in the furnace, but are as soft as lead. They still follow the standards of the world in their works and are known to lie to God by their tonsure [rite of admission to the clerical state by clipping or shaving a part of the head]. They live in twos or threes, or even singly, without a shepherd, not in the Lord's sheepfold, but in their own. Their desires are their law: whatever they think of or choose to do, they call holy, and they consider what they do not like as unlawful.

The fourth type of monks are called the Gyrovagues. These spend their whole lives moving from one province to the next, staying as guests for three or four days in different monasteries, always wandering and never stable. They obey their own wills and the entirements of gluttony, and are in all ways inferior to the Sarabites."

His son Louis became his first successor. Upon Louis's death in 840, his three sons quarreled and eventually split the empire into three parts in 843. The very names of Charlemagne's successors articulate the decline of his Frankish kingdom: Louis the Pious, Charles the Bald, Louis the Stammerer, Charles the Fat, and Charles the Simple.

Charlemagne, King and Emperor

Many scholars contend that Charlemagne, king of the Franks and first Holy Roman emperor, was the first powerful figure to emerge from the Early Middle Ages as a fully documented ruler. In The Life of Charlemagne, *Einhard, the great king's eighth-century biographer, describes Charlemagne in his later life.*

"The Emperor was strong and well built. He was tall in stature, but not excessively so, for his height was just seven times the length of his own feet. The top of his head was round, and his eyes were piercing and unusually large. His nose was slightly longer than normal, he had a fine head of white hair and his expression was gay and good-humored. As a result, whether he was seated or standing, he always appeared masterful and dignified. His neck was short and rather thick, and his stomach a trifle too heavy, but the proportions of the rest of his body prevented one from noticing these blemishes. His step was firm and he was manly in all his movements. He spoke distinctly, but his voice was thin for a man of his physique. His health was good, except that he suffered from frequent attacks of fever during the last four years of his life, and towards the end he was lame in one foot. Even then he continued to do exactly as he wished, instead of following the advice of his doctors, whom he came positively to dislike after they advised him to

During his reign, Charlemagne greatly expanded the Frankish kingdom and, by championing Christianity, converted thousands to the new religion.

stop eating the roast meat to which he was accustomed and to live on stewed dishes."

When Charles the Fat (youngest son of Louis the Stammerer) died in 888, the once-powerful kingdom fell into total disarray. The writings of ninth-century abbot Regino of Prüm offer valuable insight into the breakup of the Frankish Empire.

Lacking a legitimate heir after his death, the kingdoms which had obeyed his command dissolved their union and broke into parts. . . . Each of them decided to elect a king for itself from within the kingdom. This caused great wars, not because the Franks were lacking princes who were noble, strong, and wise enough to rule the kingdoms, but because they were so equally matched in their generosity, dignity, and power that the discord increased, because no one excelled so much above the others that they would have deigned to submit to his lordship. Frankland could have produced many princes well suited to handle the helm of the kingdom if fortune had not aroused them to destroy each other in their striving for excellence.[9]

Moreover, in the throes of disorder, the kingdoms of Europe fell prey to renewed external assaults: The seafaring Vikings invaded England and western Europe from the north; the Magyars (Hungarians) swept into Germany, France, and Italy from the east; and the Saracens (Muslims) slashed at the coasts of Provence (southern France) and Italy and vanquished Sicily and the Balearic Islands in the western Mediterranean.

The bickering—and some say inept—kings of the crumbling Frankish Empire could not provide adequate protection for their subjects. Accordingly, they turned to the powerful ruling lords of the land for help, often exchanging land in return for military assistance. Many lords constructed fortified dwellings and castles for defense against their enemies. Peasants, in turn, built their villages of huts near these castles and offered their services to the lords in exchange for protection. In this way, a new social order took root.

Thus, out of chaos, conflict, and economic decline, a revitalized Western civilization arose and matured over a millennium that came to be called the Middle Ages.

The Medieval Social Order

*F*eudalism was not a period of time during the Middle Ages but a political system. The word derives from the medieval Latin *feudum*, meaning "possession" or "property." Feudalism arose out of the chaos resulting from barbarian upheavals, fragmented states, and the absence of a strong central government capable of protecting the people. Beginning in France, the system evolved gradually between the eighth and eleventh centuries (although experts disagree on the time and place of its origin) and was instituted in some form in all the countries of western Europe.

The Feudal System

The feudal system flourished from the eleventh to the end of the thirteenth century. Few definitions of feudalism surpass that of Will Durant's in accuracy and conciseness. "Feudalism," he writes, "was the economic subjection and military allegiance of a man to a superior in return for economic organization and military protection." [10]

It is fairly common in the Western Hemisphere today for people to think of the feudal period primarily as an English experience. Yet feudalism originated and spread on the European continent at least three centuries before it was introduced in England, probably at the time of the Norman Conquest. Ebenezer C. Brewer's *Dictionary of Phrase and Fable* affirms this timing:

English feudalism is commonly held to begin with William the Conqueror [1027–1087] who acted on the principle that all land belonged to him. It was granted to the tenant-in-chief in return for homage and military service, etc., who passed on land to sub-tenants in return for other services. Thus a pyramidal social struc-

Scholars believe that William the Conqueror introduced feudalism in England.

ture developed in which every man was bound to an overlord and ultimately to the King.[11]

In a comparative sense, the so-called feudal pyramid resembles the organizational chart of a modern corporation, starting with a single block at its top, representing the chief executive officer (or king), and cascading downward and fanning out to include many blocks at its base, indicative of the lowest level of managers (or subtenant landholders).

Although approximately 90 percent of people in the Middle Ages were peasants, farmers, or village laborers, the feudal system was essentially an institutional organ of the elite, controlled and presided over by the nobility. But the system flowered or faltered on the work of the laypeople, who formed the base of feudalism's pyramidal structure and who supported, in ascending order, the lords (and their knights), overlords, and kings.

The Six Key Elements of Feudalism

History books abound with varying—often conflicting—definitions of feudalism. The same can be said of the basic components of feudalism; their identities and definitions vary greatly from source to source, both in concept and degrees of complexity. Perhaps British historian Norman Davies reaches a middle ground in identifying the six key elements of feudalism as "heavy cavalry, vassalage, enfeoffment, immunity, private castles, and chivalry."[12] These elements seem to fairly characterize feudalism and are therefore worthy of closer examination.

Heavy cavalry, Davies's first key element, required great oversize steeds, or warhorses, sufficiently sturdy and powerful enough to bear the weight of an armored knight in battle. The destrier, an expertly bred and highly trained beast, was the most valued of all warhorses; the courser was also greatly prized. Such horses originated in Persia and Byzantium and were introduced in the West by Charles Martel, an eighth-century Frankish ruler. To maintain these warhorses, Martel appropriated large amounts of church land, for which he has been credited by some as having founded European feudalism. Thereafter, as Davies suggests, a social framework was needed that could permanently sustain the services and expenses of a growing class of knights. Since land was essential to the upkeep and training of a knight, his retinue, and his horses, and since landholdings equaled wealth that needed protection, it followed that the landowner would become knighthood's benefactor in return for knightly servitude. Out of this association emerged the central theme of feudalism.

Vassalage, the second key element, was a form of indentured service in which a vassal, or subordinate, was tied to a lord, or superior, by an oath of fealty (loyalty). Vassalage began in Carolingian times (circa 613 to 987), but its roots can be traced to the old Roman practice of *commendatio*, or commendation. Out of the fealty oath (called commendation) grew the act of homage, a rite in which the vassal and lord expressed their mutual obligations. The ceremony was sealed with a kiss, which symbolically bound both for life to their sworn obligations—the vassal to serve, the lord to protect and to maintain.

The third element of feudalism, the *feodum*, or fief, was a land grant for services or fee, hence "enfeoffment," a grant of fief. It derived from the Roman practice of *beneficium*, or benefit, a lifetime land grant made to veteran soldiers. The practice carried over into Carolingian times as payment for military

In this illustration from a fourteenth-century manuscript, Charlemagne receives a feudal oath from one of his knights.

service. The term was later applied to church-owned properties assigned to individuals as a reward for their services.

As Davies points out, vassalage and enfeoffment often conflicted in actual practice. For example, a knight who was sworn to act in the interests of his lord might also possess a fief and thus feel more inclined to pursue his own interests. Such incompatibilities inevitably led, in Davies's view, to "the characteristic tensions, and treacheries, of feudal society."[13]

Immunitas, or immunity, Davies's fourth element, granted exemptions from taxes and other burdensome or restrictive measures imposed by a central authority. First extended to the church, immunity later spread to other institutions, organizations, and individuals, particularly the landholding aristocracy. These grants of immunity ultimately undermined central authority and resulted in a scattering of independent domains wherein the landed aristocracy ruled autonomously. Consequent-

ly, disparate realms promoting their own best interests, without regard for the greater good of society as a whole, became a distinguishing characteristic of the feudal order.

A more imposing characteristic of the feudal age was the fifth of Davies's feudal elements—the stone castle. Davies credits the castle, in combination with the heavy cavalry, with minimizing the destruction wrought by Viking, Saracen, and Magyar marauders. Although Byzantine armies began building castles, or "fortified places," in the mid–sixth century, castle building did not begin in western Europe until late in the ninth century. Strategically positioned atop stony crags and along barren coasts, stone castles dominated the surrounding countryside. Early on, they served several functions, providing strongholds for defense against raiders, bases for launching the outside operations of knights and men-at-arms, and safe havens for local inhabitants. Eventually, when the authority of kings and princes dwindled to near impotency, privately owned castles became bulwarks of feudal dominions and stood as rock-solid deterrents to the rebirth of central authority.

Lastly, of Davies's six key elements of feudalism, perhaps none has been dissected, analyzed, and romanticized more than chivalry. Madeleine Pelner Cosman, a lexicographer of medieval terms, defines chivalry in one sentence: "The philosophy and practice of valorous service."[14] Many others have written volumes to capture the essence of the term and all that it embodies.

Chivalry derived from the medieval French term *chivalerie*, meaning "knighthood" and "deeds of horsemanship and arms." The term originated around 1100 and basically refers to the code of values of knights—kings, aristocrats, and their *milites*, or men-at-arms. The knightly code embraced and exalted the virtues of courage, loyalty, honesty, generosity, gallantry, martial skills, and many other admirable qualities. The knight was bound by oath and conscience to defend the church, to respect and protect women and children, to aid the poor and the weak, to uphold truth and justice, to keep his word, to love his country, to honor his lord, and to fight the enemies of Christianity. In time, the meaning of chivalry grew to encompass all knightly customs and

Account of a Viking Raid

In medieval times, the mass of commoners looked to the nobility for protection against marauders. This need for protection can be readily inferred from Regino of Prüm's account of a Viking raid in 892. Reproduced in Medieval Europe, *edited by Julius Kirshner and Karl F. Morrison, his account reads as follows:*

"In the year of the incarnation of the Lord 892, in the month of February, the Northmen [Vikings] who had remained near their ships crossed the Meuse [River], invaded the district of the Ripuarians [Franks who settled near Cologne in present-day Germany], and, swallowing up everything with their congenital cruelty, arrived in Bonn. Leaving from there, they seized a village called Lannesdorf. A Christian army met them there, but did nothing worthy of being considered manful. When night came, the Northmen left the village. Because they were afraid of the enemy's onslaught, they did not dare to venture onto the flat land and fields, but constantly kept to the forest instead, left the army behind and to their left, and moved their troops as quickly as they could to the monastery of Prüm. The abbot and the congregation of his brethren barely managed to escape as they were just about to break into the monastery. The Northmen entered the monastery, devastated everything, killed some of the monks, slaughtered most of the servants, and took the rest captive. Leaving from there, they entered the Ardennes [plateau largely in Belgium, east of Meuse River] where they attacked and quickly conquered a fortification which had only recently been constructed on some high mountain, where countless people had sought security. They killed all of them, returned with their vast booty to their fleet, loaded their ships, and sailed with all of their troops back to the lands beyond the sea."

practices, including the titles, orders, rites, heraldry, and vernacular of knighthood. "In its widest sense, however, [chivalry] refers to the prevailing ethos of feudal society as a whole, which was so completely dominated by the knights and all they stood for," notes Davies. "With Christianity, it is one of the twin pillars of 'the medieval mind.'" [15]

So far, medieval society has been represented diagramatically (in terms of a pyramid and as an organizational chart) and metaphorically (in that chivalry, one of its key components, functions as "one of the twin pillars of 'the medieval mind'"). Other noted chroniclers of the medieval social order envision a third symbolic representation.

A knight and his horse dressed in war regalia. A medieval knight swore to behave by a moral code known as chivalry.

The Medieval Triangle

"Medieval culture and society persistently functioned along the lives of an identifiable structured model," writes Norman F. Cantor. Feudalism established a substantial part of the functioning social order in the Middle Ages, but by no means all of it. Cantor perceives "the continuing active medieval paradigm [model]" as threefold:

> The Nobility. Aristocratic Heroism and Militarism
>
> The Church. Hierarchic Authority and Tradition
>
> Middle Class Ethos. Sensibility and Sentiment [16]

The nobility, in Cantor's view, comprised some two to three hundred eminent families of western Europe. They monopolized most of Europe's landed wealth and controlled virtually all of the existing governmental power. Their behavioral code lionized male gallantry, martial strength, and rule by paternal—and therefore inherited—right.

The church represented a progressive institutional entity with universal influence. It not only dominated religion but led the way in learning, education, and the visual arts. Most important, the church viewed the world in hierarchical terms (that is, in terms of a descending order of superiors and subordinates based on ability or social standing). This laddered view of the world greatly influenced social structures and political systems as well as the church's own organization.

The middle class of Cantor's model included both the urban and rural bourgeois as well as the lower nobility—in England, the knights and later the landed gentry—and the more affluent and literate peasantry and arti-

Medieval noblewomen (left) and a woman from the middle class are dressed in typical garb. The aristocracy in Europe, of which the women on the left would have been part, dates from about 900.

sans. These richly diverse social groups collectively formed a cultural wellspring from which gushed a torrent of critically sound ideas and new attitudes toward faith and morality. Their fresh approaches to traditional ways of doing things marked an important stride forward in a culture and society moving steadily toward an intellectual reawakening.

"Medieval civilization may therefore be visualized as a triangle," Cantor concludes, "with the nobility's aristocratic heroism as the base and the church's hierarchic vision and middle class sensibility as the other two sides."[17] A brief examination of the base and two sides of the medieval triangle might help to illuminate how their geometrical relationship scribed the pattern for life in the Middle Ages.

The Nobility

Class distinctions date back almost to the first organized human society. In ancient times, the few ruled over the many. The few included kings and nobles, church leaders, and military chiefs; the many, the remaining mass of citizens who did most of society's work. This imbalanced division of classes held true in Roman times and carried over into medieval times. Will Durant explains:

> In the early Middle Ages there had been only two classes in western Europe: German conquerors and native conquered; by and large the later aristocracies in England, France, Germany and northern Italy were descendants of the conquerors, and remained conscious of this blood relationship even amid their wars. In the eleventh century there were three classes: the nobles, who fought; the clergy, who prayed; and the peasants, who worked. The division became so traditional that most men thought it ordained by God; and most peasants, like most nobles, assumed that a man should patiently continue in the class into which he was born.[18]

The class known as the nobility, or aristocracy, emerged in Europe about 900, following the barbarian invasions. The Plantagenets of England and the Capets of France, for example, provided ruling dynasties for several centuries.

High-ranking noblemen laid claim to titles of fanciful eminence, such as duke, count, and baron; noblewomen likewise claimed corresponding titles of rank—duchess, countess, and baroness. They lived lives of privilege and plenty that only money and power can attain and sustain. "They owned, by one legal mechanism or another, at least eighty percent of the arable land in Europe," declares Professor Cantor. "They ruled over millions of dependent peasants—usually serfs [members of a servile class] bound to the land."[19]

The favored status of the nobility spawned responsibilities, however, often described as noblesse oblige—literally, nobility obligates—or the obligation of honest, generous, and responsible behavior associated with high rank or noble birth. An obligation to protect and provide for their dependents ranked as one of the paramount responsibilities of the nobility. This protection entailed the need for an ongoing military capability, as Cantor observes:

> Whatever else the aristocracy did—in politics, religion, art, and literature—it was military valor and personal strength and courage that had originally made the great noble families powerful in society, and this physical prowess was continually necessary to sustain their position in society. Centered with their landed wealth and political authority as the basis of medieval society, the nobility could effectively and subtly interact with the other sides of the medieval triangle, the church and the middle class. But heroism and military honor had to be maintained if the nobility was to continue its fundamental role. The glamor of heroism, the training for fighting, the struggle for domination—these conditions remained essential to the life of the nobility, no matter the more peaceful and intellectual ingredients that eventually became included in their mind-set and behavior.[20]

In short, those incapable of defending what was theirs during the Middle Ages would soon find themselves with little or nothing to defend. Moreover, beyond the defense of their own domains, nobles were morally bound to defend the Roman Catholic Church, the single institution that stood for the common good.

The Church

Many scholars believe that the spirit of the church and its work—primarily, providing spiritual guidance and furthering education and the arts—represented the great civilizing influence of the Middle Ages. But its influence did not come easily. After the fall of Rome, the church's authority alternately increased and decreased for several centuries. "One of the primary points to remember about the church in the Middle Ages is that its policy and power changed drastically and rapidly," writes Sherrilyn Kenyon, an authority on medieval life and an assisting editor for the *Medieval Chronicle*. "There were times when the church's power was weak and other times when it was strong."[21]

The strength of the church in large measure depended upon a solid alliance with a powerful authority outside its own religious hierarchy. The church exhibited great strength in Germany and France, for example, because those countries welcomed and supported the presence of papal influence. Where the church was unwanted, however, its influence was correspondingly weak.

Christianity was established throughout the Roman Empire and the Middle East during the first two centuries after the death of Christ. Two cities more than any others greatly influenced and guided church affairs: Rome and Constantinople (now Istanbul).

The church withstood many controversies between Eastern and Western factions. Though it split temporarily in 867, it quickly reunited and remained unified under the pope in Rome for nearly two more centuries. In 1054, however, the patriarch in Constantinople refused to yield to the will of the pope, and the Great Eastern Schism split the two factions into the Roman Catholic Church and the Eastern Orthodox Church. They remain separated to this day.

Because the pope was elected to office by the college of cardinals (the members of which rank directly below him in the ecclesiastical hierarchy), he reported to no lay authority, as did the patriarch, who was appointed by the emperor. Archbishops, who oversaw provinces, were ranked below cardinals, followed in turn, in descending order, by bishops, who oversaw dioceses; the regular clergy comprising friars, monks, and nuns; and the secular clergy of laybrothers and stewards.

Members of the nobility routinely held the higher offices of the church. According to Norman Cantor:

At any given time during the Middle Ages at least three-quarters of the bishops and other upper echelons of the medieval clergy came from the nobility, whereas the same proportion of the parish clergy derived from peasant families. The bishops shared much of the outlook of their brothers and cousins in the lay nobility about heroism and militarism, and between the eighth and twelfth centuries fighting bishops who buckled on armor and wielded a sword were not uncommon. Yet the church officials comprised a distinctive group in medieval society with their own view of the world. Their outlook and behavior were separate from the secular aristocracy, even though bishops, abbots, and cardinals normally stemmed from families of the higher nobility.[22]

Such differences in outlook and behavior inevitably led to discord. "Throughout the period, arguments were made and policies were changed regarding the church's authority," adds Kenyon. "In fact, the reality of papal supremacy,

A monk preaches to his flock. Monks were at the bottom of the church hierarchy, though they had the most contact with members of the church.

though an idea as old as the first century, wasn't effectively claimed until the Gregorian reforms of the late eleventh century." [23]

Historians traditionally credit Pope Gregory VII with championing the reform program of the eleventh century. He worked hard to amend many facets of secular (nonclerical) control over the church. And he worked with equal diligence to reform clerical morals, forbidding priests to marry and

enforcing his edict by depriving some dissenters of their parishes and excommunicating others. But his main efforts were directed against the practice of investiture—that is, the right of lay sovereigns to confirm or ratify church offices.

"But for all Pope Gregory VII's reforms, he still ended his life deposed and deprived of the papal throne," concludes Kenyon. (In 1084, a clerical council of his antagonists ex-

Dictates of the Pope, 1075

In 1075, Pope Gregory VII banned lay (nonclerical) investiture, that is, the right of the emperor and other princes to appoint abbots and bishops and invest them with the ring and staff that symbolized their office. By issuing his Dictates of the Pope, *Gregory VII started a controversy between church and state that lasted until a compromise was reached in the Concordat of Worms in 1122. A part of his* Dictates, *excerpted from Bryce D. Lyon's* The High Middle Ages, *is shown here.*

"That the Roman church was founded by God alone,

That the Roman pontiff alone can with right be called universal.

That he alone can depose or reinstate bishops.

That, in council, his legate [agent], even if a lower grade, is above all bishops, and can pass sentence of deposition on them. . . .

That for him alone is it lawful, according to the needs of time, to make new laws, to assemble together new congregations, to make an abbey of a canonry;

and, on the other hand, to divide a rich bishopric and unite the poor ones.

That he alone may use the imperial insignia.

That of the pope alone all princes shall kiss his feet.

That his name alone shall be spoken in the churches.

That his is the only name in the world.

That it may be permitted to him to depose emperors. . . .

That no chapter and no book shall be considered canonical without his authority.

That a sentence passed by him may be retracted by no one; and that he himself, alone of all, may retract it.

That he himself may be judged by no one. . . .

That the Roman church has never erred; nor will it err to all eternity, the Scripture bearing witness. . . .

That he who is not at peace with the Roman church shall not be considered catholic."

communicated Gregory and removed him from the papal throne. His spirit broken, Gregory died in exile in 1085.) "And even with his reforms, most of the following popes had a difficult time enforcing them."[24]

According to London-based author James Harpur, a specialist in medieval subjects, the argument over lay investiture raged on after Gregory's death in 1085:

> Eventually a compromise was reached in the Concordat of Worms in 1122. It was agreed that the church, not the emperor, should elect bishops and abbots and invest them with the ring and the staff, symbols of their spiritual authority, while the emperor could invest them with the scepter, the symbol of secular authority.[25]

The perpetuation of the church's hierarchical view of the world formed the basis of its orthodox theory. Clerics believed wholeheartedly in their superiority over laypeople and in their right to dictate to the laity. The pope, they felt, was superior to *all* laypeople—including kings and emperors. Spiritual rule, then, rightfully took precedence over secular power. Such are the views that the church traditionally tried to implement and that led to centuries of discord between church and state.

In assessing the effectiveness of the church's hierarchical authority and tradition, Norman Cantor concludes: "Overall, orthodox theory fell far short of full implementation, but the dominant theory persistently affected group and individual behavior."[26] Indeed, by the thirteenth century, despite an abundance of shortcomings, the church became the strongest single influence in Europe. The pope possessed more power and wealth than all the lay sovereigns and nobles combined, and the great mass of people again looked to Rome for spiritual guidance and salvation.

The Middle Class

During the Early Middle Ages and part of the High Middle Ages, only two classes of people existed in the secular world under the feudal system—the nobility and the peasantry. But, as Will Durant points out, "The economic revolution of the twelfth century added a new class—the burgesses or *bourgeoisie*—the bakers, merchants, and master craftsmen of the towns. It did not yet include the professions."[27]

Following on the heels of the economic revolution, western Europe experienced a population explosion during the first three-quarters of the thirteenth century. The rapid population growth produced a land shortage in many areas. This shortage of land had a twofold effect: It stimulated improvements in farming techniques and farm equipment designed for more efficient use of the land, and it caused a population shift, forcing many peasant farmers to seek other means of livelihood in towns and cities.

"By 1200, the middle class, consisting of the burghers [bourgeois, those who lived in a *burg*, a fortified town] in the cities and the gentry (lower nobility) and yeomen (wealthy peasants) in the countryside, comprised at least a quarter of the medieval population," estimates Norman Cantor. "They were hardworking, enterprising, ambitious people." All three qualities served them well, for, as Cantor emphasizes,

> they did not inherit great estates and fancy titles like the aristocracy. They did not live off official positions like churchmen. Even though occasionally a fortunate gentry family would rise into the aristocracy, and even though the middle class provided most of the personnel of the church below the top rank of the

Dressed in the garb that indicates their class, two merchants (left) converse with a nobleman (right). The middle class emerged in the twelfth century.

hierarchy, the middle class had a distinct consciousness that they—burghers, gentry, yeomen—were fundamentally separate from both the aristocracy and the churchmen. They were a distinctive force in me-

dieval Europe, an identifiable unique side to the medieval triangle.[28]

And there can be little doubt about the huge contributions the medieval middle class made to the advancement of civilization. By the start of the fourteenth century, for example, much of the European economy owed its burgeoning success to an early form of capitalism, motivated by a craving for profit no less passionate than that of today's Wall Street brokers. In the cities and new towns that sprang up in medieval Europe, rife with commerce and industry, a new breed of affluent bourgeois began to introduce the ideas and cultural changes that would help shape the face of today's Western civilization. Clearly, the middle class was highly deserving of taking its place as the third side of the medieval triangle.

In summary, the nobility ruled, protected, and provided for its subjects; the church provided spiritual guidance and fostered the continuance of education and the arts; and the bourgeoisie, with its collective ambition, enterprise, and hard work, paved the road to modern times. The medieval social order, along with geographical location, largely determined the quality and character of life during the Middle Ages.

Rural Life

Rural life in feudal times centered on expansive country estates called manors, especially on the fortified castle or manor house of the resident landowning lord, or landlord. The lord owned or managed the estate, and the peasants worked the land in return for the lord's protection. In terms of individual rights and freedom, as applied chiefly to eleventh- and twelfth-century England and France, the people who made up the manorial community belonged to one of three groups.

Freemen, Slaves, and Serfs

Focusing primarily on medieval England and France, then, society consisted of freemen, slaves, and serfs. Freemen comprised nobles, members of the clergy, knights and men-at-arms, people of professional standing, most merchants and artisans, and a few peasants who either owned their land free, or nearly free, of ties to a feudal lord or leased it from a lord for a moneyed fee. In eleventh-century England such peasant proprietors made up some 4 percent of the farming population. Their ranks swelled substantially in southern France, western Germany, and northern Italy, where their numbers totaled somewhere close to 25 percent of the peasant population in western Europe.

At that time slavery was already declining, and it diminished further as serfdom grew. Slavery flourished in Germany during the tenth century, primarily because of the availability of pagan Slav captives and the willingness of privileged Germans to enlist them to work on estates or offer them for sale in the Byzantine or Muslim slave markets. By the twelfth century, however, the use of slaves in England was pretty much limited to domestic service, and north of the Loire River in France, slavery was almost nonexistent.

Slavery's decline resulted not from moral enlightenment but from the exigencies of a changing economy. Quite simply, slavery—that is, forced labor—proved more troublesome, less productive, and considerably less profitable than production motivated by an acquisitive urge and the prospect of self-betterment.

Although the slave never disappeared completely from the medieval workforce, it was the serf who filled Europe's breadbaskets with grain during the Middle Ages. *Serf* derives from the Latin *servus*, a term that was at first used interchangeably for both serf and slave but eventually changed into *serf* and was no longer used to refer to an individual subservient to a dominating master.

The feudal system stood on the shoulders of the serf, who worked to support his lord. Technically, a serf was "unfree," that is, he was bound to the land but not to any given lord who held the land in fief (since possession of a fief was subject to change). Although he was not owned by another person, as was the slave, the serf could not leave his birthplace. But neither could a lord force him to leave. So, the serf typically tilled a plot of land owned by his lord, paying an annual rent in produce, labor, or money in return for a lifetime of tenure and military protection. Upon the serf's death, his tenured land passed to his heirs only at the pleasure and consent of the lord.

A wide divide separated freemen from serfs, but the gap separating serfs and slaves was comparatively narrow. Thus, in practical application, feudal class distinctions were essentially reduced to two groups: the ruling class and the working class.

Members of the ruling class and their household staffs resided in castles and manor houses, whereas peasants of the working class lived in huts clustered about the lord's dwelling for protection or clumped together in nearby villages, but usually within the walls of the manorial settlement.

In a sixteenth-century illustration, a serf pays rent to his feudal lord. Though not a slave, a serf was tied to the manor and could not leave it.

The Medieval Castle

The castle, perhaps more than anything save the knight, has come to symbolize the Middle Ages. Although castles appeared in the Byzantine Empire and in Islamic countries as early as the sixth century, castle building did not commence in western Europe until late in the ninth century, probably in France. Once begun, castle building spread quickly to other areas. But it was not until the twelfth and thirteenth centuries, after the crusaders returned from fighting Islam in the Middle East, that European castles began to equal their Byzantine and Islamic counterparts, both in size and grandeur.

Early European castles—crudely built of timber and earth but effective in defense—were known as motte-and-bailey castles. Jean de Colmieu, an early chronicler, describes the building of a motte this way:

It is the custom of the nobles of the neighborhood to make a mound of earth as high as they can and then encircle it with a ditch as wide and deep as possible. They enclose the space on top of the mound with a palisade [fence] of very strong hewn logs fixed together, strengthened at intervals by as many towers as they have means for. Within the enclosure is a house, a central citadel or keep which commands the whole circuit of defense. The entrance to the fortress is across a bridge . . . supported on a pair of posts . . . crossing the ditch and reaching the upper level of the mound at the level of the entrance gate [to the enclosure].[29]

During peaceful periods, the lord and his family resided in the castle keep, an inner stronghold or defensive tower perched on top of the mound. The rest of the castle's occupants—knights, squires, grooms, members of the domestic staff, and others—along with horses and other livestock lived in wooden structures in the bailey, or courtyard, below. When under attack or siege, everyone took shelter in the keep.

During the later Middle Ages, castles became more elaborate in design and more enduring in construction. Many medieval castles remain standing today. In the High and Late Middle Ages, they formed the core of rural life in England and western Europe.

"Though many castles were built inside towns for political and strategic reasons, the castle was rooted economically in the countryside," write Joseph and Frances Gies, authors acclaimed for their work in popularizing medieval history. Continuing, the Gieses lace together the basic elements of rural living:

[The castle] was connected intimately with the village and the manor, the social and economic units of rural Europe. The village was a community, a collective settlement, with its own ties, rights, and obligations. The manor was an estate held by a lord and farmed by tenants who owed him rents and services, and whose relations with him were governed by his manorial court. A manor might coincide with a village, or a village might contain parts of manors or several entire manors.

The manor supplied the castle's livelihood. The word "manor" came to England with [William] the Conqueror, but the arrangement was centuries old. On the Continent, it was used to provide a living for the knight and his retainers at a time when money was scarce.[30]

Castle Living Arrangements

"Few medieval descriptions survive of the old motte-and-bailey castle, and only one gives information about living arrangements," assert historians Joseph and Frances Gies. In Life in a Medieval Castle, *they include medieval chronicler Lambert of Ardres's description of a timber castle hall built on a motte at Ardres, Flanders, early in the twelfth century.*

"The first story was on the ground level, where there were cellars and granaries and great boxes, barrels, casks, and other household utensils. In the story above were the dwelling and common rooms of the residents, including the larders, pantry and buttery and the great chamber in which the lord and lady slept. Adjoining this was . . . the dormitory of the ladies in waiting and children. . . .

In the upper story of the house were attic rooms in which on the one side the sons of the lord of the house, when they so desired, and on the other side the daughters, because they were obliged, were accustomed to sleep. In this story also the watchmen and the servants appointed to keep the house slept at various times. High up on the east side of the house, in a convenient place, was the chapel, decorated like the tabernacle of Solomon. . . . There were stairs and passages from room to room, and from the house into the gallery, where they used to entertain themselves with conversation, and again from the gallery into the chapel."

While the lord (or king) might keep a few knights in residence to guard himself and his family from routine dangers, the cost of feeding, clothing, and equipping a knight forced the typical lord to minimize his staff of live-in protectors. "For this reason," explains historian Joseph Dahmus, "the king normally gave lands (benefice or *precarium*) to most of these vassals [knights], who were then expected to provide for their own maintenance from what resources these lands returned."[31]

In this way knights became landholders, and titles to their lands eventually (after a few generations) became inheritable to successive heirs, perpetuating the descendant pyramidal levels of the feudal system. Nevertheless, each lord, within budgetary constraints, trained and retained as many knights as possible to defend his realm. Knights formed a vibrant and vital part of life in a castle.

Castle Life

"By the thirteenth century life in a castle was far from spartan," notes historian Philip Warner, a lifelong student of castles and military history. "Furniture was still minimal, but aumbries (cupboards) had been made in walls, and there were plenty of chests for storing clothes and other goods." Adds Warner:

> Crusaders and traders had brought tapestries and carpets back from the Middle East. Paint was always bright, and even the exterior of castles glittered in the sunlight. Glass was available but scarce. Some attempt was made to sweeten the atmosphere: herbs were strewn on the floor and occasionally lavender and other sweet-smelling seeds were left in bowls, as they still are at certain castles today, but more as tokens than necessities.

Benches or forms [long seats] were good enough, if not too good, for ordinary people, but there were a few chairs for those worthy of them. The most important person at any meeting took the chair and by merely occupying that position indicated his authority.[32]

Life in a castle represented a study in communal living, as many of today's students of the medieval age have observed. "The most striking thing that we would notice about domestic life in the Middle Ages, even for the rich, would be the general lack of privacy," observes British author John Guy. "Much of daily life (including administrative and judicial matters) was carried out in the hall [of the castle], which acted as a communal eating and living room." Then, as now, the wealthy held a premium on life's comforts and pleasures, as Guy observes:

> The level of domestic comfort was quite high, with ample provision of fireplaces. . . . Lighting was by candle or oil lamp.
>
> The rich ate very well, meals consisting of 10 or more courses. Royal banquets might extend to several hundred courses! Food was often decorated, or "disguised," after cooking, such as pushing feathers back into a pheasant to resemble the live bird.
>
> Much of the tableware was made of metal, such as silver or pewter. . . . Nobles considered pottery and earthenware should be used only by the lower classes.
>
> Evening meals lasted several hours and were often accompanied by musicians. Jesters, jugglers and acrobats might entertain between courses. . . .
>
> There was no shortage of variety in the food eaten at a lord's table which might

Mounted knights emerge from the castle of their feudal lord as a few of the lord's serfs look on. Though only the lord and his family lived in the castle full-time, during periods of war it housed the lord's knights and others tied to the manor.

include beef, mutton, pork, poultry (or other birds such as starlings, pigeons or gulls), vegetables, fruit, cheese, soup, fish, herbal salads and bread, followed by ale or wine. Herbal infusions were the usual hot drinks. . . . Knives and spoons were the only cutlery used.[33]

Beyond merely providing living comforts and pleasurable pastimes, affluence also opened the door to learning and the perpetuation of the cultured lifestyle of the privileged class. Among the nobility, boys received preferential treatment. Boys were given a formal education, whereas girls were tutored in the home in domestic duties and crafts, such as embroidery and sewing. Yet many girls became literate and often entertained their families with readings from the Bible and epic tales. Sons were usually trained to be knights or courtiers (court attendants); daughters faced a choice between early marriage— usually at about age fourteen—or the nunnery.

If a young woman opted for marriage, she would likely experience many days like this one described by Sherrilyn Kenyon:

An average day for a noblewoman might include attending morning mass, grabbing a quick bite to break the fast, meeting with servants to instruct them on special duties for the day, meeting with the steward [manager of the estate] and other officials, overlooking accounts and records, and breaking for the midday meal at noon. If guests were present, she'd spend the rest of the day entertaining them with hunting trips, hawking, singing, or some other planned festivity. Otherwise, she'd check on the servants, and make sure the children were attending their lessons. In the absence of her husband, she would also be expected to hear complaints and even rule in legal matters. In the event of an attack, she would lead the castle's defense.[34]

The role of the noblewoman, ostensibly subordinate to that of her spouse, bears a striking similarity to her husband's functions in castle life. Compare, for example, James Harpur's description of a day in the life of a nobleman:

> A typical daily routine for a nobleman would start at dawn with Mass in the chapel. He would then take a light breakfast before attending to the affairs of the day, such as the administration of his estates. A large meal was served at about midday, after which he might go off on a hunt—usually deer—or perhaps hawk, ride, or fence. Supper was served after sunset, accompanied by singing in the Great Hall's gallery. After dinner entertainment on some days might include jugglers, acrobats, singers, and harpists.[35]

The lord and his lady usually retired early. Responsibility for preparing the lord for bed fell to the chamberlain. A medieval manual for household management outlines the chamberlain's duties to his lord like this:

> Take off his robe and bring him a mantle to keep him from cold, then bring him to the fire and take off his shoes and hose . . . then comb his head, then spread down his bed, lay the head sheet and the pillows, and when your sovereign is in bed, draw the curtains. . . . Then drive out the dog or cat, and see that there be basin and urinal set near your sovereign, then take your leave mannerly that your sovereign may take his rest merrily.[36]

Noblewomen performed many of the same duties as their husbands, including instructing the servants and entertaining the castle's guests.

Thus ended a typical day in the life of a nobleman. A typical day in the life of a peasant was similar in length but in little else.

Village Life

The mass of peasantry, largely serfs representing the base of the medieval pyramid, resided in villages housing anywhere from ten to sixty or more families. The peasant built his own house. He first constructed a frame of heavy branches and post, then filled in the walls with wattle—a structure of interwoven sticks and twigs—and mud. Residents of colder climates often opted to build a sod house. In both instances, the roof was thatched.

Inside of what was generally a one-room cottage, occupants made do with a floor of well-trodden earth, sometimes covered with layers of straw or reeds and usually fouled by pigs, chickens, and other domestic animals housed with the family. Doors and shuttered windows allowed access and furnished light in the daytime, but all were securely fastened against possible nighttime intruders. A crude hearth provided heat and means for cooking. Until fireplaces and chimneys gained prominence in the Late Middle Ages, a hole cut near the top of the dwelling close to the gable sufficed to evacuate smoke.

Roasted Peacock

Medieval recipes often contained more detailed instructions than typical modern recipes. In The Medieval Reader, *for example, historian Norman F. Cantor includes the following extract from a fifteenth-century English cookbook. These directions for roasting a peacock leave little to chance.*

"Take a peacock, break its neck, and cut its throat, and flay [strip] it, skin and feathers together, with the head still attached to the skin of the neck, and keep the skin and the feathers whole together. Draw the bird like a hen, and keep the bone to the neck whole, and roast it. And set the bone of the neck above the spit, as the bird was wont to sit when it was alive, and bend the legs to the body, as it was wont to sit when it was alive. And when it is roasted enough, take it off and let it cool, and then wind the skin with the feathers and the tail about the body, and serve as if the bird were still alive; or else pluck it clean and roast it and serve it as you do a hen."

The peasant's sparse, rough-hewn furnishings typically included a plank table on trestles, a few benches and stools, perhaps a chest for valuables, and usually a loom for the women to make cloth. The family slept on one bed, most often a pile of dried leaves or straw strewn on the earthen floor.

Peasant women made all of the family's clothes, mostly of wool or linen. A typical wardrobe started with a tunic, a hip-length or longer blouse or jacket with a round neck and narrow sleeves; it was tied around the waist with a leather cord and worn by both men and women. A cap, long hose, and flat leather shoes without heels completed the peasant's attire. In the summer, the peasant often went barefoot or wore wooden clogs. No one wore underwear or nightclothes until the Late Middle Ages.

"In the early medieval period there was surprisingly little difference between the clothes worn by men and women," declares John Guy. Wardrobes of the wealthy contrasted with those of the workers primarily in quantity and variety of fabric. "The length of a person's over-tunic (cotte) showed their status," continues Guy. "Poor people wore them to the knee, merchants to the calf, clergy and professional classes to the ankle."[37]

Only the rich, of course, could afford jewelry and expensive accessories, which further distinguished the upper class. Wardrobes became more elaborate with the addition of "new, more exotic and colorful materials, such as silk and printed cotton,"[38] imported from the Middle East by the end of the fifteenth century. In sum, those who could spent a lot of money on clothes; those who could not, did not.

The diets of the lower and upper classes contrasted much more sharply than did their wardrobes. Most peasants cultivated a small garden plot to augment the commodities grown in the larger fields, raising cabbage, onions, peas, beans, turnips, and other such diet enhancers. Pungent herbs like mustard, sage, garlic, and parsley added flavor and flair to the peasant's fare, inexpensive substitutes for the costly imported spices often found gracing the lord's table in the castle or manor house, the likes of which few peasants could afford.

Gruel, a thin porridge, represented the main staple in the peasant's diet, with dark breads of rye or barley running a close second. For meat, the peasant relied mostly on salt pork, with perhaps a fowl on special occasions and, fortuitously, despite heavy penalties for poaching, an infrequent game bird or animal. Fish formed a small part of the peasant diet, either angled for in nearby ponds or streams or bought at a local market; eggs and a variety of cheeses supplied most of the protein. The choice of beverages depended on location and climate: predominately wine from grapes in southern locales, and beer from barley and hops, or mead—a fermented brew made of water, honey, malt, and yeast—in northern climates.

The Good Earth

Although the populace of the manorial village included some tradespeople—such as masons, cobblers, tailors, millers, smiths, bakers, butchers, and other food processors—the vast majority of villagers worked the land. Remarks James Harpur:

> Medieval peasants, as one contemporary expressed it, licked the earth, ate the earth, spoke of the earth, and placed all their hopes in the earth. If most peasants were to some degree in servitude to a feudal superior, their relationship with the earth was even more binding: to the earth they owed their existence. The overriding concern of life—beset as it was with the threat of drought, crop blight, and famine—was to produce enough food to eke out a meager existence.[39]

In many areas of western and northern Europe, farming was concentrated in vast, open fields surrounding or adjacent to the lord's manor. Prevalent crops included grains—wheat, barley, oats—and peas, beans, and other legumes. Domestic animals—pigs, cows, oxen, horses, sheep, chickens, and so on—were raised and grazed on common land and helped to maintain the manorial estate's self-sufficiency. Since hay fodder reserves were usually not adequate to sustain all of the livestock over a full winter, many of the animals were slaughtered in the fall and preserved in salt for future consumption.

Peasants toil in the fields, reaping and sheaving grain. Some manors required hundreds of peasants to maintain and harvest crops.

John Ball recruits peasants to revolt against their lords in 1381. Ball was later executed for his efforts to achieve justice for the peasants.

The farmlands were divided into three large fields. Serfs were assigned rights to strips of land—usually distinguished by stone markers—in each field. This so-called three- or open-field system assured that no single person would hold either the best or poorest land parcels. Land reserved for the lord was called the *demesne*. Peasants worked the lord's land for two or three days a week and their own land for the remainder of the week. They worked the open fields together, from spring planting to fall harvesting, volunteering draft animals and equipment in a cooperative effort.

For most peasants the work was grueling and the returns were small. Yet throughout the feudal period the majority of the peasantry remained faithful to their lords and to the good earth. But their loyalty waned toward the end of the High Middle Ages.

Leaving the Land

In England, a growing rancor among the peasantry was evidenced by the Peasants' Revolt of 1381, directly occasioned by an unpopular tax. John Ball, one of the rebel leaders who was later executed, echoed the resentment of his peers in his appeal to a rebellious audience:

> What have we deserved, or why should we be kept thus in servage[?] We all be come from one father and one mother, Adam and Eve. Whereby can they say or showe that they be greater lords than we be, saving by that which they cause us to win and labour for that they dispende? They are clothed in velvet and chamlet [soft leather] furred with grise, and we be vestured with pore clothe; they have their wynes, spyces and good bread, and we have the drawings out of chaffe and drink water. They dwell in fair houses, and we have the pain and travail, rain and wind in the fields. And by that which cometh of our labours, they kepe and maintain their estates.[40]

Clearly, all was not well between the upper and lower classes. As early as the eleventh century, peasants began leaving the countryside in ever-increasing numbers, seeking to improve their lots and their fortunes in the burgeoning cities of medieval Europe. Such migrations accelerated the growth of a new class of commoners called burghers.

CHAPTER 3

Urban Life

During the eleventh and twelfth centuries, the growth of towns in number and size in western Europe began transforming the shape of the previously mostly rural medieval society. Writer and editor James Harpur, an authoritative voice in the fields of archaeology, history, mythology, and religion, proposes the following reasons for such growth:

> Their rise can be attributed to various factors: a period of peace after the depredations of the Vikings [in the late ninth century and beyond] and other warrior peoples and an increase in population—itself partly due to an improvement in agricultural techniques, food production, and diet.[41]

Then, as now, periods of political calm and social stability stimulated trade. Wealthy merchants began establishing offices in towns and constructing permanent storehouses to keep up with the increasing demands for their goods. Increased sales brought greater profits, contributing in turn to both the revitalization of old communities and the birth of new ones. Opportunities for work abounded, steadily attracting large numbers of both free and bound peasants from the surrounding countryside. A flux of small traders, peddlers, and vagrants streamed into towns and cities.

As towns grew larger, community leaders attempted to organize towns as self-governing entities, in effect detaching themselves from feudal ties and obligations. Such efforts to sever their feudal connections put them at opposition with authorities—kings, princes, clerics, and nobles—who held the properties upon which the towns were raised.

In due course, town leaders applied to authorities to buy a charter that permitted them to establish a commune—a usually self-governing settlement organized on the basis of collective ownership and use of goods and property. (The term *commune* is sometimes used to connote the political body consisting of an assembly of citizens and a cadre of officials that together regulate the affairs of a city.) The charter empowered them with not only the right of self-government but the right to make laws, mint money, bear arms, and assess taxes. Feudal overlords no doubt at first frowned at towns striving to become autonomous. But their disdain was likely soon appeased by the benefits derived from their newly imposed taxes and tolls, and the goods and services supplied by the towns.

Despite the benefits that nobles and clerics acquired from towns, conflicts of authority continued to occur, sometimes giving rise to riots and other rowdy behavior. As an example, Harpur cites the case of the bishop of Laon, who tried to suppress the town's commune in 1112.

> In order to do so, he had to buy the king's permission; and to recoup his money, he, in turn, tried to impose a severe tax on the town. The result was a riot. A lynch mob

found the bishop quaking in a wine barrel and butchered him.[42]

Such events occurred frequently during extended periods of social change and civil unrest. People across Europe, from Italy to England, often rebelled against the oppression and exploitation of lords and church officials.

Opening the Trade Routes

Despite the church's tendency toward occasional misuses and abuses of its authority, it continued to permeate and affect all aspects of medieval life. As one form of reverence, devoutly religious Christians of all classes routinely journeyed to religious shrines in far-off places—the grave of a martyr, for example, or the site of a significant religious happening. In spite of the dangers and difficulties of traveling great distances, Christians flocked in droves each year to their favorite shrines. A pilgrimage to the holy city of Jerusalem represented the ultimate devotional act for a Christian.

Even though Arabs had ruled the Holy Land for several centuries, they had allowed Christians to make their pilgrimages unmolested. But when the Holy Land fell to the Seljuk Turks in the eleventh century, the Turks soon began persecuting Christian pilgrims. In 1095, Pope Urban II rallied Christian knights and soldiers to defend the Cross. "God wills it.

A medieval marketplace teems with activity. Merchants ply their wares and a beggar (bottom left) appeals to the shoppers, while players (upper left) perform for the crowds.

Christ himself will be your leader when you fight for Jerusalem,"[43] he cried.

Thereafter, commencing at the end of the eleventh century and continuing for the next two hundred years, the Roman Catholic Church championed a series of eight religious wars called the Crusades. In the end, the Crusades failed to permanently regain the Holy Land for Christians. Long military expeditions from western Europe to the Middle East, however, reopened overland avenues of trade and revitalized sea routes between East and West.

After experiencing firsthand the wonders of a higher level of civilization in the East—a society better educated and governed, richer and more advanced in architecture and in the arts and sciences—crusaders returned home with new ideas, new customs, and a new vision for the future. Twelfth-century crusader and cleric Fulcher of Chartres, amazed by the size and wealth of Constantinople upon seeing the city for the first time, wrote:

Oh what a fine and noble city! What monasteries, what palaces it has, what amazing workmanship! How many marvellous works even in the streets and suburbs! It would take too long to relate the wealth of all manner of goods there, of gold, silver, all types of clothes and holy relics. For merchants sail all the time bringing necessities there.[44]

The Death of the Bishop

"At Laon [France] in 1115 [sources vary as to the year] citizens took advantage of their corrupt bishop's absence to establish a commune," recounts historian Will Durant in The Age of Faith. *"On his return he was bribed to take oath to protect it; a year later he induced King Louis VI to suppress it."* To illustrate *"the intensity of the communal revolution"* that followed, Durant provides the following excerpt from an account written by Guibert of Nogent, a twelfth-century monk.

"On the fifth day of Easter week . . . there arose a disorderly noise throughout the city, men shouting 'Commune!' . . . Citizens now entered the bishop's court with swords, battle-axes, bows, hatchets, clubs, and spears, a very great company. . . . The nobles rallied from all sides to the bishop. . . . He, with some helpers, fought them off with stones and arrows. . . . He hid himself in a cask . . . and piteously implored them, promising that he would cease to be their bishop, would give them unlimited riches, and would leave the country. And as they with hardened hearts jeered at him, one named Bernard, lifting his battle-ax, brutally dashed out the brains of that sacred, though sinner's head; and he, slipping between the hands of those who held him, was dead before he reached the ground, stricken by another blow under the eye-sockets and across the nose. There, brought to his end, his legs were cut off, and many another wound was inflicted. Thibaut, seeing a ring on the bishop's finger, and not being able to draw it off, cut off the finger."

After slaughtering the bishop, the enraged and crazed citizens set the cathedral ablaze and razed it. They then turned to looting and flaming the homes of the aristocracy, until a royal army united with nobles and clergy to storm the city and massacre the populace en masse.

Crusaders and Muslims face off in the first battle of the First Crusade. Though the Crusades did not succeed in defeating the "infidels," the battles did succeed in reopening trade with the East.

Nothing in Frankish Europe compared with the Byzantine capital. But the Crusades, if nothing else, reopened trade with the East, which created new wealth in the West. New wealth, in turn, accelerated the growth of new villages and towns and hastened the expansion of existing cities, such as the future great cities of London and Paris.

The Rise of the Middle Class

The growth of towns and cities eventually led to the emergence of a new kind of urban citizen, variously termed burghers, burgesses, or bourgeoisie—that is, the middle class. By the close of the 1100s the communal system had firmly established itself in western Europe. Although cities rarely attained total independence, they succeeded in slipping the yoke of

their feudal overlords, ending or reducing tariffs, and severely limiting clerical rights.

The new mercantile middle class held sway over community and economic affairs. Guilds, that is, associations of merchants or craftsmen akin to today's unions, gained recognition as self-governing entities. In some instances the guild and the commune (the body politic governing the city) were one and the same. More often, however, the two functioned separately, and the commune seldom interfered with guild interests.

"Now, for the first time in a thousand years, the possession of money became again a greater power than the possession of land," observes Will Durant. "Nobility and clergy were challenged by a rising plutocracy [a controlling class of the wealthy]."[45]

As might be expected, the nobility resented the erosion of their wealth and authority by a newly rich class of commoners. The working class at the bottom of the social ladder found little to celebrate as well. Although workers enjoyed more personal freedom under the new communal system, most remained poor, only now they were subservient to the new mercantile class rather than to the old aristocracy.

A Burgher's House

The comfortable lifestyle of the affluent middle class rivaled that of the aristocracy, without many of the obligations incumbent upon those of noble rank. As a case in point, Renard Le Contrefait, a fourteenth-century clerk of Troye, France, once described life among the burghers this way:

> They live very nobly, they wear a king's clothes, have fine palfreys [saddle horses, as distinguished from workhorses or warhorses] and horses. When squires go to the east [crusading], the burghers remain in their beds; when the squires go get themselves massacred, the burghers go on swimming parties.[46]

During the thirteenth century, urban houses of both rich and poor looked pretty much the same from the outside. "Except for a few of stone, they are all timber post-and-beam structures, with a tendency to sag and lean as they get older," write Joseph and Frances Gies. Inside urban houses, similarities between rich and poor tended to disappear. The Gieses explain:

> In the poor quarters several families inhabit one house. A weaver's family may be crowded into a single room, where they huddle around a fireplace, hardly better off than the peasants and serfs of the countryside.

A well-to-do burgher family, on the other hand, occupies all four stories of its house, with business premises on the ground floor, living quarters on the second and third, servants' quarters in the attic, stables and storehouses in the rear. From cellar to attic, the emphasis is on comfort, but it is thirteenth-century comfort, which leaves something to be desired even for the master and mistress.[47]

In a typical burgher's house, a steep flight of stairs off the ground-floor anteroom led to a large hall, or solar, on the second floor. Equivalent in many ways to the great hall of a castle, the solar served as a combination living and dining room. A blazing fire under the hood of a great chimney provided most of the room's lighting, day and night, but was supplemented at night with oil lamps and an occasional candle. Since most candles were made from animal fat that was both costly and time-consuming to accumulate, the mistress of the house usually conserved candle use, limiting them to church and ceremonial functions.

The large, low-ceilinged solar was generally spare and often held a chill beyond the fire's warming reach. Panels of linen cloth, dyed and sometimes embroidered, adorned the walls and reflected the mistress's handiwork and personality. Rushes strewn about the floor substituted for carpeting, which was rarely used in thirteenth-century Europe. Sparse but functional furnishings usually included a long trestle table that was disassembled after meals, several benches, a large wooden cupboard containing dishes and silver, and a low buffet for storing everyday pottery and tinware. Chests and cupboards were crudely constructed on posts, with planking nailed lengthwise sufficing for sides.

Of the second-floor rooms, the spacious kitchen ranked next to the solar in importance. Kitchen activities, as described by the Gieses, revolved around a huge walk-in fireplace. Built back-to-back with the solar hearth, it shared the same chimney. A great iron kettle supported by a toothed rack from the hearth kept water continually heating over a fire that was rarely extinguished. Additional kettles and cauldrons stood nearby on tripods. Ladles, skimmers, spoons, pokers, long-handled forks, and various other cooking utensils hung before the fireplace. A garbage pit, emptied periodically, was also located close by, as was a huge vat containing the household water supply.

Garden herbs—basil, rosemary, sage, savory, and thyme—were hung to dry in bunches from overhead beams. Exotic and expensive spices such as saffron, cinnamon, ginger, and nutmeg were kept in a locked wall cupboard. A long worktable, butted against the wall beneath the spice cupboard, provided space for preparing the burgher's culinary favorites.

Above the kitchen and solar were the family bedrooms. The master and mistress of the house slept in a massive canopied bed—often as large as eight feet in length and seven feet in width—with a straw-filled mattress strung

The comfortable home of a middle-class man. Note the rush floor mats, large fireplace, and elaborate decor.

on rope suspenders. Typical bedding consisted of linen sheets, wool and fur blankets, and pillows stuffed with feathers. Children's beds were much smaller and covered with serge and linsey-woolsey, a coarse fabric of wool and linen or cotton. Even in the wealthier homes, residents waged an incessant battle against fleas, bedbugs, and other vermin.

In some homes, when the need arose to answer nature's call, residents could look forward to a long walk to the privy located behind the house with the stable and storehouses. A few homes had a private room off the bedroom called a *garderobe*, equipped with a chute to a vessel in the basement that was emptied periodically.

"Even for a well-to-do city family, making life comfortable [was] a problem. But," conclude the Gieses, "arriving at a point where comfort becomes a problem for a fair number of people is a sign of advancing civilization."[48]

City Streets

While inside their homes, wealthy merchants maintained a fair level of opulence compared with that of poor workers, but in public all levels of medieval society shared the city streets without distinction or favor. Over time, succeeding generations have come to regard medieval cities as quaint and romantic. But as Will Durant so aptly puts it, "We must not idealize the medieval town."[49] By romanticizing the medieval city from a latter-day perspective, its coarser realities often escape consideration or mention.

Most medieval streets were little more than narrow, winding alleys, designed for easy defense and shade. Wooden-shoed men and women and heavy-footed beasts vied for rights of passage over twisting, bustling lanes, amid a chorus of shouts and clattering

hoofs. In an age without machines, the pace was slower but more tiring.

Many city dwellings retained a countrified ambience, with surrounding gardens, chicken coops, pigpens, cow pastures, and dunghills. Such pastoral scenes prompted London, a city perhaps more sensitive to urban blight, to decree: "He who will nourish a pig, let him keep it in his own house."[50] But citizens of most cities grew impervious to the sight of swine rooting freely about the open garbage heaps.

Occasionally, heavy rains turned the streets to mud for days on end. Men wore boots to slog through the mud; ladies in their finery were transported about town in chairs or carriages. While a few, more enterprising cities paved their major thoroughfares with cobblestones in the thirteenth century, most streets remained unpaved, smelly, and unsafe.

Most thirteenth-century towns and cities were walled to defend against marauding nobles. But protection came at a high price. "Although the wall served its purpose until the fifteenth century, when gunpowder made it possible for cannon balls to breach its thickness, the physical security was gained at a heavy social and psychological price," writes Norman Cantor. "The wall that kept the robber barons out also crammed the houses together along crooked, filthy streets and exacerbated the burghers' proclivity to mass paranoia."[51] Forced to huddle behind protective walls and unable to roam freely in neighborhoods beset with crime, townspeople no doubt at times felt trapped in a prison with no prospect of parole.

Crime and Punishment

In medieval society, as in all societies before and after, poverty and squalor sometimes fostered unlawful activities, but not as often as some might expect. "The popular notion of lawlessness in the Middle Ages is largely unfounded," ventures historian John Guy. "Most petty crimes were tried through local courts, usually by the lord."[52] A brief glimpse of medieval crime and punishment supports Guy's contention.

The Crown controlled all courts but generally concerned itself only with serious felonies. Such crimes were referred for a hearing before judges who toured the country on a regular quarterly schedule. Conviction of a felony—such as murder, but sometimes an offense as benign as petty theft—usually resulted in a death penalty. The condemned were executed by beheading, hanging, or burning at the stake.

A medieval judge arbitrates a disagreement between a peasant and a merchant. Appointed by the Crown, such judges toured the villages on a regular basis.

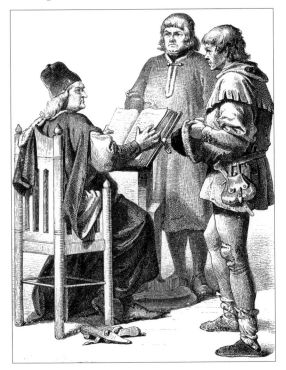

Law enforcement and peacekeeping duties fell to shire reeves, or sheriffs. Although the poor were allowed to seek help, such as money, food, or lodging, from the church, anyone arrested for begging could expect a flogging or a stint in the stocks as punishment. A stock was a device for publicly punishing offenders, consisting of a wooden frame with holes in which the feet, or feet and hands, could be locked. Offenders were also often humiliated by being bound and paraded through the streets in a cart. Because most crimes were punished by fines, by compensating victims, or by execution, few prisons were needed.

After dark, most city streets' lighting was nothing more than an occasional candle or lamp in a window. This minimal illumination did little to deter those disposed to break the law. Consequently, at dusk, most prudent city dwellers found it beneficial to rush home to the safety of their houses. Cathedral bells heralded curfew at eight or nine in the evening, which served as a signal to cover fires with ashes to reduce the chances for house fires during the night. Most families retired for the night shortly after curfew.

The Middle-Class Family

The middle-class family of the Late Middle Ages was not unlike today's typical family of middle-income means. Nor did the roles of a burgher and his spouse and children differ greatly from those of a suburban lord and lady and their offspring. They ate rich foods, wore fine fabrics and adornments, indulged in fun pastimes—miracle plays, fairs, festivals, and so on—and generally became better educated, all in the manner of the nobility.

"The upper level of the Third Estate [commoners], made up of merchants, manufacturers, lawyers, office-holders, and purveyors to

Medieval Punishment

In 1326, Queen Isabella of England led a bloody revolt against the tyrannical reign of her husband, King Edward II. Shortly after seizing the throne, she exacted swift punishment against two of the king's closest advisers, Hugh Despenser the father and Hugh Despenser the son. In Chronicon de Lanercost, 1201–1346, *the Lanercost chronicler describes the fate of the Despensers. The following extracts from the* Chronicon *are taken from* Chronicles of the Age of Chivalry, *edited by Elizabeth Hallam.*

Queen Isabella led a successful revolt that ended the reign of her husband, King Edward II.

"Queen Isabella and her army left Gloucester and hurried to Bristol, which was held by Hugh Despenser the father. . . . Although the place was well defended, Hugh Despenser the father was overcome with the despair that so often afflicted his party, and opened the gates of the city, throwing himself and his adherents on the mercy of that harridan [shrew].

The city and castle were thus surrendered to that virago [loud, overbearing woman] the queen, who entered and at once, without another word, gave orders that Hugh be made to suffer the most extreme torture. At once, that brave knight was bound, his legs and arms stretched, his belly was torn open and his very intestines were cruelly ripped forth and burnt. The rest of his body was drawn by horses and then hung on a fork like that of any common thief."

Hugh Despenser the son was subsequently captured in the abbey at Neath and sometime later called before the queen at Hereford.

"Then Hugh Despenser the son was brought forth in chains, his eyes blazing terribly at this indignity, for he held no hope of being tried fairly according to the proper procedure.

And indeed, here, at Hereford, he was drawn, hanged, beheaded and cut into quarters. His head was sent to London Bridge and the four quarters of his body were sent forth to the four quarters of the kingdom."

A husband and wife prepare their wares—poultry and eggs—to take to the market. A wife often had much to do with the relative success or failure of the family business.

the crown, had nothing left in common with its working-class base except the fact of being non-noble," notes the eminent American historian Barbara Tuchman. "To overcome that barrier was every bourgeois magnate's aim."[53]

To this end, middle-class men of wealth and power managed businesses, practiced professions, and held forth in the political arena or at court. The success of a business often owed much to the magnate's spouse. Notes Tuchman:

> Management of a merchant's household— of his town house, his country estate, his business when he was absent—in addition to maternal duties gave his wife anything

but a leisured life. She supervised sewing, weaving, brewing, candle-making, alms-giving, directed the indoor and outdoor servants, exercised some skills in medicine and surgery, kept accounts, and might conduct a separate business as *femme sole* [as if she were a single woman].

Some women practiced as professors or doctors even if unlicensed.[54]

Children of the affluent middle class, particularly boys, often studied for one of the professions. Others were apprenticed to a trade. Girls, like their country counterparts, were usually schooled in the domestic arts.

Mercantile Power and Prosperity

As can be seen in the study of earlier and later societies, money buys political power. During the later Middle Ages, wealthy merchants used their money to buy city charters and install themselves as governmental leaders, enabling them to make the laws and set the standards. In short, they used their wealth to buy total control over their cities or towns. But the power of the affluent mercantile middle class was not always wielded to the great benefit of the working class, as Will Durant points out:

> Even more than in antiquity the mercantile *bourgeoisie* turned its wealth, energy, and ability to political advantage. In most cities it eliminated the poor from assemblies or offices. It oppressed the manual worker and the peasant, monopolized the profits of commerce, taxed the community heavily, and spent much of the revenue in internal strife, or in external wars to capture markets and to destroy competitors. It tried to suppress artisan [trade] associations, and refused them the right to strike, under penalty of exile or death. Its regulation of prices and wages aimed at its own good, to the serious detriment of the working class.

"But all in all, the work of the medieval communes did credit to the skill and courage of the businessmen who managed them," Durant concedes. "Under their leadership Europe experienced in the twelfth and thirteenth centuries such prosperity as it had not known since the fall of Rome."[55]

Money and the Growth of Trade

While the quality of feudal life had been predicated on land ownership, the quality of communal life in the fourteenth century was measured in money. Commenting on "the power of money," in the mid-1300s, Spanish writer Juan Ruiz opined:

> Money can do much; it should be held in high esteem. It turns a tramp into a respected and honorable man; it makes the lame man run and the dumb man speak. Even a man without hands reaches out and grabs for money. A man may be an idiot or an ill-bred peasant, but money will make him a noble and a sage; the more money a man has, the more worthy he becomes, while the man who is penniless cannot call himself his own master. If you have money, you can have luxury, pleasure, and joy, and benefices [ecclesiastical appointments or rewards in return for clerical duties] from the Pope; you can buy Paradise and earn salvation. Piles of money bring piles of blessings.[56]

It is likely that most members of the affluent middle class held an abiding interest in eliminating the social barrier separating them from the nobility. Making a pile of money and continually adding to the pile probably seemed to them like an excellent way to end the class distinctions inherent in the feudal system.

The Birth of Credit and the Shift of Mercantile Power

In 1350 two landmark developments in European finance and commerce helped immeasurably in speeding the decline of feudalism. First, negotiable credit instruments were created, which enabled the acquisition of money by means of a written promise of future payment. And second, the preponderance of mercantile power shifted from the Mediterranean to northwestern Europe, namely, from Italy to the Netherlands and England. These two countries subsequently dominated the European economy well into the industrial age. Of these developments, John H. Munro of the University of Toronto, an authority on medieval commerce and finance, writes:

> The two developments were very closely related: throughout the medieval and early modern era merchants controlled banking; and supremacy in international banking and finance was almost always the consequence of commercial hegemony [dominance of leadership, particularly by one nation over another], especially in long-distance trade. When Italian merchants were gaining that ascendancy, they were also creating the fundamental instruments of modern banking; and subsequently Netherlandish and English

merchants, during their rise, perfected the techniques of negotiability and vastly expanded the role of credit.[57]

And as historian Robert S. Lopez so knowingly asks, "Is not buying and selling on credit the very essence of commerce?"[58]

Moneylenders and Trading Centers

The use of hard money originated at least four thousand years ago, but standardization of money or coinage did not follow until about 700 B.C. Many scholars credit Lydia, a city-state in Asia Minor, with issuing the first coins, crudely designed and roughly shaped ingots of electrum, a mixture of gold and silver. Barter, the exchange of one commodity for another, proved wholly inadequate to the advance of commerce and yielded to a standardized, convenient medium of exchange.

Under feudalism, great lords and highly ranked clerics exercised the right of coin mintage, but during the High and Late Middle Ages, governments all but monopolized the coining of money. By 1284 all major European nations minted a reliable gold coinage, with the exception of England. During the reign of Henry II (1154–1189), England issued silver coins, valued as the most stable currency in Europe. Gold coinage eventually arrived in England in 1343.

During the twelfth and thirteenth centuries, the church, with an extraordinary facility for raising funds and maintaining their liquidity, became the greatest financial power in Europe. "From her wealth the Church lent money to persons or institutions in difficulty," writes

Workers busily mint coins. Originally the responsibility of lords, coin making was controlled by governments in the late thirteenth and early fourteenth centuries.

Will Durant. But because "these loans by church bodies were usually for consumption or for political use, seldom for financing industry or trade,"[59] the professional financier became the principal source of finance capital. These financiers, or moneylenders, provided funds for the before-profit costs of an enterprise. Moneylenders harkened back to the money changers of ancient times, but, rather than simply changing money, they invested their own and other people's money in enterprises or extended loans to churches, nobles, and kings.

With the rejuvenation of trade during the Crusades, new streams of commerce flowed inland and northward from the great seaports of the Mediterranean—Genoa and Pisa in Italy; Marseilles in France; Barcelona in Spain. Mercantile power underwent a shift northward. Trade thrived. Merchants—the new middle class—began accumulating great wealth. Comments historian James Harpur:

> In northern Europe, trading centers flourished in the valleys of rivers such as the Rhine and Seine, which saw the expansion of Cologne and Mainz, and Paris and Rouen, respectively. Honey, fish, and furs were typical northern commodities. Wool manufacture was an important industry in the Netherlands where, in the Flemish towns of Ghent, Ypres, and Bruges, weavers worked their looms to make cloth from wool brought over from England. In time, English towns such as Norwich and Winchester developed their own cloth industry and rivaled their counterparts across the water.[60]

Much of the business of trade and commerce was conducted at fairs, uniquely medieval commercial institutions where goods could be sold or exchanged. "Most fairs evolved from a village or town market which

A moneylender works with clients in the center of a medieval fair. Such men were the earliest bankers, issuing loans and credit.

by some happy circumstance, usually its accessibility, began to attract merchants and goods from distant provinces and countries," writes historian Joseph Dahmus. "When this happened the king or local lord might grant a special charter and declare it a fair." Fairs dated back to the fifth century, notes Dahmus, but became "especially popular and useful in the twelfth and thirteenth centuries when they served as the principal emporia for commodities from distant provinces and countries."[61]

The most famous and prosperous of these fairs were held six times a year in the Champagne region of northeastern France. Of the Champagne fairs, James Harpur writes:

These fairs lasted 49 days and merchants traveling to them enjoyed the protection of the local lords in return for payment. Merchants from England brought bales of wool on the backs of mules; those from Germany came with furs and linens; and Spanish traders arrived with leather goods. The last week of the fair was spent settling accounts; and the moneychangers [moneylenders] who gave loans and credits became known as bankers from the benches, or "banks," on which they used to count their coins.[62]

Moneylenders—such as the Cahorsians, a powerful group of lenders based in Cahors, in southern France—sometimes deservedly earned reputations for engaging in unfair or corrupt practices. For example, Matthew Paris, a thirteenth-century English monk, wrote:

In these days (1235) the abominable plague of Cahorsians raged so fiercely that there was scarcely any man in all England, especially among the prelates, who was not entangled in their nets. The king was indebted to them for an incalculable account. They circumvented the indigent in their necessities, cloaking their usury [lending money at excessively high interest] under the pretense of trade.[63]

Most moneylenders, however, performed a valuable and honest service. But, as Will Durant points out, "it was the Italians who developed banking to unprecedented heights in the thirteenth century."[64]

The Great Merchant Bankers of Italy

Many banking functions that remain in practice today can be traced back to the Babylonians of 2000 B.C. The Romans refined some of these practices and added more in the heyday of their empire. But it was during the High

Middle Ages that the greatest advances in banking methods were made—and they were made in Italy.

"The world," declared Pope Boniface VIII in 1300, "is made up of five elements: earth, air, fire, water—and Florentines."[65] With these flattering words, he honored the great Florentine merchant-banking firms whose agents and practices so enormously influenced "the shifting currents of international trade."[66] But substance, rather than exaggeration, motivated his declaration.

Indeed, existing records show that eighty Florentine banking firms existed between 1260 and 1347. Along with the great money firms of Genoa and Venice, Florentine bankers, "in or before the thirteenth century, developed nearly all the functions of a modern bank."[67] Many of their banking innovations would give today's lords of commerce pause to wonder how it was possible to conduct business prior to the thirteenth century.

Italian bankers accepted deposits and carried open accounts that enabled a smooth exchange of funds between parties engaged in ongoing money transactions. The Bank of Venice, for example, arranged exchanges between client accounts through simple bookkeeping procedures as early as 1171. They loaned money secured by items of value—jewelry, art objects, expensive armor, government bonds, and the like—and sometimes on entitlements to public funds. They also bonded goods for transfer out of country.

The Italians developed an international banking network that allowed them to issue letters of credit, which enabled a deposit to be made in one country and redeemed in another by the depositor or his designee, a device used by earlier moneylenders.

Bankers also wrote bills of exchange, whereby a merchant could give a promissory note in return for goods or a loan and defer payment to the creditor until a stated date.

An illustration from a fourteenth-century manuscript depicts the interior of an Italian banking establishment. The Italians established the modern bank.

These notes were eventually balanced against one another at a bank or at one of the great trade fairs. Money changed hands for the first time only when the final balance was paid. Hundreds of such exchanges could now be accommodated in this manner, free of the weight and bother of carrying great sums of money over great distances. Writes Will Durant:

> As the banking centers became clearing houses, the bankers avoided the long journey to the fairs. Merchants throughout Europe and the Levant [the eastern shores of the Mediterranean Sea] could draw on their accounts in the banks of Italy, and have their balances settled by interbank bookkeeping.

"In effect, the utility and circulation of money were increased tenfold," Durant contends summarily. "This 'credit system'—made possible by mutual trust—was not the least important or honorable aspect of the economic revolution."[68] Another equally important element of the "revolution" was the establishment of the guilds.

The Guilds

A guild is an association of people with similar interests or pursuits. Guilds of one sort or another existed in the Byzantine and Roman Empires. During medieval times, separate and diverse groups of merchants and craftsmen banded together according to their common interests "in order to maintain standards and support its members."[69] The eleventh-century resurgence of trade renewed interest in guilds.

While the quality of a product fixed wages and prices, guilds set standards for workmanship. Guild members underwent an apprenticeship to become journeymen. A guild mastership was awarded to a journeyman usually only after long years of experience, and then only after the member produced a masterpiece of workmanship deemed worthy by the guild. Much like today's unions, the guilds provided protection and benefits for its members. Not all workers formed guilds, however, for varying reasons. In some instances, the king or lords would not allow them, as indicated by historian Sherrilyn Kenyon:

> The reasons for the guilds are multitudinous. Guilds gave the towns power to barter their freedom from the lords or king who ruled them to form their own laws. As a result of this power, there were also towns who never had guild merchants. Some lords refused to relinquish control.[70]

Specialized craft guilds represented a wide range of skilled artisans. Weavers, dyers, goldsmiths, leather workers, butchers, carpenters, bakers, masons, brewers, fishmongers, harness makers, hatters, cartwrights, cobblers, tailors, and many more craftsmen united in separate associations. Most guilds maintained strong religious ties. Many adopted patron saints and gave generously to church charities and building funds.

In addition to craft guilds, merchants organized into their own powerful fraternities. Members of merchant guilds specialized in buying and selling goods and commodities and engaged in wholesale trade with far-off places. Many of these guilds accumulated enormous wealth and strongly influenced city governments. "The guilds of the wealthier traders tended to become political pressure groups rather than economic bodies,"[71] asserts Robert S. Lopez. Perhaps the most powerful of all mercantile guilds was the Hanseatic League that dominated the Baltic cities for centuries.

Customs of the Guild of St. Omer

Medieval guild members gathered regularly for traditional social and religious ceremonies. Many such gatherings culminated in a "drinking feast," in which the consumption of distilled spirits played an important role. The "Customs of the Guild" of twelfth-century St. Omer, France, reflect the necessity for closely regulating personal behavior at these affairs. The following "customs" are extracted, in part, from Medieval Europe, *edited by Julius Kirshner and Karl F. Morrison.*

"When the time for the drinking-feast is approaching, the law is that the doyens [senior members] summon the members of the guild to their chapter-meeting on the day before the feast. There they command the guild members to come in peace to their seats at the ninth hour [between about 2:00 and 3:00 P.M.] and to keep peace with each other concerning both old and recent deeds.

If someone insults the doyens, he shall give two ounces of silver.

If someone insults anyone else and two people have heard it, he shall give half an ounce.

If someone hits anyone with a fist, a loaf of bread, or a stone, since no other weapons are available, he shall give two ounces.

If someone rises up in anger from his seat against another, he shall give one ounce.

If someone carries a cup filled with drink out of the guildhall without permission, he shall give half an ounce.

For every insult in deed or word that is committed during the two days of the feast one must answer to the doyens, and no other judge."

Emerging from the Viking Age (circa 800–1066), when Vikings regularly raided the coastal areas of northern Europe and pirated shipping in the North and Baltic Seas, merchants along the Baltic Sea banded together for protection and formed *hansas*, or commercial associations. The first *hansa* was established at Wisby, on the island of Gotland, in 1161. Many others followed. Eventually they united in a loose alliance called the *Bund van der dudeschen hanse*, or Hanseatic League, with the German city of Lübeck as its center of operations. By the fourteenth century, more than one hundred cities belonged to the league, stretching from Belgium to Poland.

"In the early days, the League aimed to consolidate the legal rights of anchorage, storage, residence, and local immunity, which its members required to conduct their business," writes Norman Davies, a scholarly chronicler of European affairs. "It was also concerned to stabilize currency and to facilitate the means of payment."[72] In protecting the interests of their members, however, the league soon became involved in politics.

"The League's original weapon lay in the *Verhansung* or 'commercial boycott' of its enemies," continues Davies. "But it was gradually obliged to levy taxes and to raise naval forces, first to suppress pirates and then to contest the policies of established kingdoms, especially Denmark."[73]

At the height of its power, the Hanseatic League, or Hansa, played a key role in preserving law and order, advancing trade with remote lands, and encouraging the free exchange of ideas throughout northern Europe. Its influence weakened by quarrels among its member cities, the league began a slow decline toward the end of the fourteenth century. Most cities had deserted the alliance

by 1630. But the cities of Bremen, Hamburg, and Lübeck continued to be known as Hansa cities until late in the nineteenth century.

Guilds were frequently criticized for their repressive and restrictive policies, much as some people reprove present-day unions. But it is fair to say that, in the larger picture, guilds performed a worthwhile, if sometimes self-serving, function in the later Middle Ages. As Robert Lopez purports, the trade guild "only partly succeeded, at the price of

The Hanseatic League

— Land Trade Routes
···· Hanseatic Sea Routes
○ Member-towns of the Hanseatic League
● Other Towns of Commercial Importance

Reval
Wisby
Sweden
Riga
North Sea
Denmark
Gotland
Baltic Sea
Königsberg
Lübeck
England
Hamburg
Lynn
Bremen
Bristol
London
Magdeburg
Poland
Bruges
Ghent
Dortmund
Winchester
Ypres
Cologne
Rouen
Laon
Mainz
Paris
Vienna
North Atlantic Ocean
Cahors
Venice
Marseilles
Genoa
Florence
Pisa
Spain
Barcelona
Corsica
Rome
Balearic Islands
Sardinia
Sicily
Messina
Mediterranean Sea

restrictions, some of which may have hindered initiative and growth. But in as far as it succeeded, it prevented the commercial revolution from inflicting on the workers the sufferings which were to accompany the beginning of the Industrial Revolution."[74]

With regard to mercantile guilds, Will Durant concludes: "They took a leading part in politics, dominated many municipal councils, effectively supported the communes in their struggles against barons, bishops, and kings, and themselves evolved into an oppressive oligarchy of merchants and financiers."[75]

As guild members accrued riches and gained power, resentment began to grow among members of the less-fortunate lower class, leading to the class wars of the thirteenth and fourteenth centuries. Nonetheless, to borrow a pair of phrases from Durant, the guilds sustained the "freedom and dignity of work" for "a bright moment"[76] in time. But that bright moment turned dark all too soon.

Prices and Change

The new mercantile wealth contributed largely to a chain reaction of events that produced dramatic changes that would profoundly and adversely affect medieval life for multiple generations. A slow increase in the European population that began in 1050 almost imperceptibly activated the chain.

Over the years, women had become comfortably acclimated to a protracted period of stability and prosperity, which encouraged them to have more children. In the twelfth century, their increased fertility resulted in a baby boom that lasted for many years. The disproportionate ratio of more dependent children to fewer productive adults increased alarmingly. Moreover, according to economic historian David Hackett Fischer,

this happened at the same time that people needed more food, fuel, houses and land. Demand for life's necessities expanded more rapidly than supply could increase. Inexorably, prices went up.[77]

In brief, as Fischer explains the inflationary spiral, the population expansion produced an expansion of trade, which stimulated industrial development. The growth of commerce and industry accelerated the amount of money in circulation, adding a monetary inflation to the preexisting supply-demand inflation.

Prices continued to rise. When governments added new money to the economy to help curb inflation, the value of money decreased. Prices soared. Wages fell. By 1320 wages had decreased by some 25 to 40 percent from a century earlier. At the same time, rent and interest increased. Even governments sank deep into debt by mid- and late century. Notes Fischer:

The first years of the fourteenth century were a time of dark foreboding for the suffering peasantry of Europe. The economy of the Western world was in deep disorder. Material inequalities had dangerously increased. The growth of population far outpaced the means of its subsistence. Poverty and hunger increased in many parts of the Western world.[78]

By the start of the fourteenth century, money and the growth of trade had ended feudalism and spawned a prosperous mercantile society. Thereafter, however, largely through overpopulation and its resultant chain-reaction effect on the economy, much of Europe plunged deep into depression. And the worst period in the history of medieval Europe was set to begin.

Famine, Pestilence, War, and Death

Given the calamities that beset most of Europe during the Late Middle Ages, many Europeans of that era must have feared that the end of the world was close at hand. Because the church formed one side of the medieval triangle and influenced all levels of society, the apocalyptic (prophetic) vision described in the Book of Revelation (6:2–8) no doubt took on an awesome immediacy for the mostly Christian populace.

According to the last book of the Bible, Jesus revealed to his bond servant John the evils to come at the end of the world, personified as four figures on horseback. The figures represented famine, pestilence, war, and death. They have become widely known as the Four Horsemen of the Apocalypse. Figuratively speaking, they began galloping roughshod over Europe early in the fourteenth century. Famine, the first of the four abominable equestrians, rode in on a black horse behind the driving rains that drenched Europe's fields and drowned its crops for three successive years.

Famine

"In the summer of 1314, the weather turned cold and very wet," notes David Hackett Fischer. "Rain fell incessantly." Crops either rotted in the fields or fell far short at harvest. King Edward II immediately imposed price con-

trols on farm products. "These disturbances seemed at first to be merely another routine disaster of a sort that had often afflicted medieval Europe," adds Fischer. Europeans had become accustomed to crop failures and short harvests. "In the winter of 1314, people tightened their belts and prayed for better times."[79]

But the following year occasioned more of the same heavy rains. Historian Barbara Tuchman recounts their tragic effects:

> In 1315, after rains so incessant that they were compared to the Biblical flood, crops failed all over Europe, and famine, the dark horseman of the Apocalypse, became familiar to all. The previous rise in population had already exceeded agricultural production, leaving people undernourished and more vulnerable to hunger and disease. Reports spread of people eating their own children, of the poor in Poland feeding on hanged bodies taken down from the gibbet. A contagion of dysentery prevailed in the same years. Local famines recurred intermittently after the great sweep of 1315–16.[80]

Further evidence of these horrors can be gleaned from the *Life of Edward II*, an account contemporary with the so-called Great Famine of 1315–1316:

> Certain portents [omens] show the hand of God was raised against us. For example,

Albrecht Dürer's famous woodcut, entitled The Four Horsemen of the Apocalypse. *The horsemen represent hunger, war, plague, and death. Dürer was no doubt inspired by the fact that the horsemen regularly visited his countrymen.*

in the previous year, there was such heavy rain that men could scarcely harvest the corn or bring it safely to the barn.

In the present year [1315] worse happened. Floods of rain rotted almost all the seed, so that the prophecy of Isaiah seemed to be fulfilled, that "ten acres of vineyard shall yield one little measure and thirty bushels of seed shall yield three bushels." [Isaiah 5:10] In many places the hay lay so long under water that it could neither be mown nor gathered. Sheep everywhere died and other animals were killed by a sudden plague.

More of the same—only worse—prevailed in 1316, as the continuing account of Edward's life reveals.

After Easter, the dearth of corn was much increased. Such a scarcity had not been seen in our time in England, nor heard of for a hundred years. A measure of wheat was sold in London for forty pence [up eightfold in price], and in other less thickly populated parts of the country, thirty pence was a common price.

Indeed during this time of scarcity a great famine appeared, followed by a severe pestilence, of which many thousands died in different places. I have even heard it said by some that in Northumberland, dogs, cats, horses and other unclean things were eaten. For there, on account of the frequent raids of the Scots, work is more irksome, as the accursed Scots despoil the people daily of their food.[81]

The total death toll attributable to the Great Famine of 1315–1316 is not known, because many deaths went unreported or unrecorded or both. Many historians estimate that the famine and associated diseases wiped out at least 10 percent of the European population. (Europe's population at that time cannot be assessed with certainty but probably stood at about 70 million people.)

To add to Europe's fourteenth-century misery, the plague that had devastated the populace from 747 to 750 reappeared exactly six centuries later. Pestilence, the second of the Four Horsemen, swept in from China in company with the Black Death.

In this medieval illustration, a victim of the plague shows the doctor his symptomatic bubo. The Black Death ravaged Europe, irrevocably changing medieval society.

population of most of the continent and England within three years. According to historian Norman Davies, the pandemic

Pestilence

In October 1347, a merchant ship from the Crimea put in to the port of Messina, Sicily, with dying oarsman pulling at its oars. The bodies of the rest of the crew and passengers lay scattered about the decks, already dead and decomposing. "When the Messinans were lifting the corpses off the vessel, they noticed that the bodies had large black swellings in their armpits and groins," writes historian James Harpur. "It was the ominous coloration of these lumps that would later give rise to the name of the Middle Ages' most deadly plague: the Black Death."[82]

Thus began a scourge that swept across Europe in whirlwind fashion, decimating the

was fuelled by a devastating brew of three related diseases—bubonic plague, [septicemic] plague, and pneumonic or pulmonary plague. The first two variants were carried by fleas hosted by the black rat; the third, airborne variant was especially fast and lethal. In its most common bubonic form, the bacillus *pasteurella pestis* caused a boil-like nodule or bubo in the victim's groin or armpit, together with dark blotches on the skin from internal hemorrhage. Three or four days of intolerable pain preceded certain death if the bubo did not burst beforehand.[83]

Although infection and contagion were not unknown to practitioners of medieval medicine, in the case of the plague, doctors failed to grasp how the disease was transmitted. They could render little in the way of effective treatment beyond offering compassion and words of hope to victims of the dreaded malady. Meanwhile, overcrowded dwellings and horrid sanitation, particularly in the cities, contributed immeasurably to an exploding rat population. Consequently, the death toll soared out of control.

"The medieval doctor was confronted with a situation where a large number of people died suddenly and inexplicably in a given area," writes Philip Ziegler, a British historian widely known for documenting the causes and effects of the Black Death. To portray a malady so disgusting "that the sick became objects more of detestation than pity," he recalls the words of nineteenth-century historian J. P. Papon to depict the disease's loathsome symptoms: "All the matter which exuded from their bodies let off an unbearable stench; sweat, excrement, spittle, breath, so fetid as to be overpowering; urine turbid, thick, black or red." Ziegler goes on to lament the doctor's plight:

This zone of mortality shifted constantly but gradually, conquering new territory and abandoning old. Any rational being, faced with such a phenomenon but totally unversed in medical lore, would be likely to arrive at the same explanation. There must be some vicious property in the air itself which travelled slowly from place to

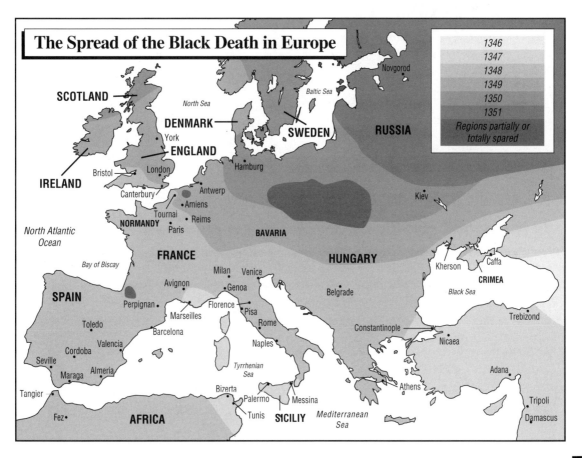

The Spread of the Black Death in Europe

1346
1347
1348
1349
1350
1351
Regions partially or totally spared

SCOTLAND
North Sea
Baltic Sea
Novgorod
DENMARK
York
SWEDEN
RUSSIA
ENGLAND
Hamburg
Bristol
London
IRELAND
Antwerp
Canterbury
Amiens
Kiev
Tournai
Reims
NORMANDY
Paris
BAVARIA
North Atlantic Ocean
FRANCE
HUNGARY
Bay of Biscay
Milan
Venice
Kherson
Caffa
Avignon
Genoa
CRIMEA
SPAIN
Belgrade
Black Sea
Perpignan
Florence
Pisa
Trebizond
Toledo
Marseilles
Rome
Barcelona
Constantinople
Valencia
Naples
Nicaea
Cordoba
Seville
Almeria
Tyrrhenian Sea
Adana
Maraga
Bizerta
Athens
Tangier
Palermo
Messina
Tripoli
Fez
AFRICA
Tunis
SICILIY
Mediterranean Sea
Damascus

place, borne by the wind or impelled by its own mysterious volition. There were many different points of view as to the nature of this airborne menace, its origin, its physical appearance. But almost every fourteenth-century savant [person of specialized knowledge] or doctor took it for granted that the corruption of the atmosphere was a prime cause of the Black Death.[84]

Additional symptoms of the so-called Black Death included coughing and sneezing, "hence the somewhat improbable suggestion that the nursery rhyme:

Ring a ring o' roses,
A pocket full of posies,
A-tishoo! A tishoo!
We all fall down.

was some form of folk memory of the Black Death."[85] In any event, the Black Death depopulated western and central Europe between 1347 and 1350, resulting in the deaths of about 25 million people, about a third of Europe's inhabitants. And even as millions died from famine and disease, the third horseman on his red steed rode rampant in the land, slaughtering untold millions more during the medieval millennium.

The Black Death in England

The plague known as the Black Death, which originated in central Asia in the 1330s, arrived in England in 1348. In the following extract from Elizabeth Hallam's Chronicles of the Age of Chivalry, *fourteenth-century chronicler Geoffrey le Baker relates how the disease began at once to take its toll.*

"All England suffered from this sore affliction so that scarce one in ten of either sex survived. As the graveyards were not big enough, fields were chosen where the dead might be buried.

Only a few nobles died, but of the common folk, more died than could be counted, and also a multitude of monks and other clerks known only to God. The pestilence struck the young and the strong in particular, generally sparing the old and the weak. Scarcely anyone would dare touch a person who was afflicted, and the remains of the dead, which in ages before and since have been held in high honor,

were then shunned by the healthy, for they were tainted with the plague.

Men who had one day been full of life, were often found dead the next. Some were afflicted with abscesses which erupted in various parts of their bodies, and which were so hard and dry, that even when they were cut with a knife, hardly any liquid flowed out. Many who suffered from these symptoms survived, either by having the boils lanced or by waiting with great endurance for them to subside. Others had small black sores which developed all over their bodies. Only a very few who suffered from these survived and recovered their health.

Such was the great plague which reached Bristol on 15 August, and London around 29 September. It raged in England for a year or more, and such were its ravages, that many country towns were almost emptied of human life."

Warriors and War

In a sense, the history of the Middle Ages is the history of war, for wars were virtually ongoing. From the wars of Charlemagne (742–814) to the campaigns of Charles the Bold (1433–1477), practitioners of the battling-and-warring profession rarely suffered from lack of gainful employment during medieval times. Of all warriors great and tall perhaps no combatant has ever equaled the fame and idolatry of the medieval knight. *The Book of Lancelot of the Lake* eulogizes the first knights in noble terms:

> In the beginning . . . no man was higher in birth than any other, for all men were descended from a single father and mother. But when envy and covetousness came into the world, and might triumphed over right . . . certain men were appointed as guarantors and defenders of the weak and humble.[86]

This passage implies, of course, that the appointees were men of noble character and purpose. Yet, in his beginnings, the knight belied the chivalric image of such glowing perception. Historian Frances Gies's description of an early knight makes this point:

> In his person, the real-life knight of the tenth century had little in common with the courtly heroes of the Round Table. Ignorant and unlettered, rough in speech and manners, he earned his living largely by violence, uncontrolled by public justice that had virtually disappeared. Civil disputes and criminal cases alike had ceased to be adjudicated by the enfeebled royal power and instead were settled with the sword. The unarmed segment of the population, the Church and the peasants,

A medieval knight takes a death thrust to the gut while attempting to fend off attack. Knights fought the medieval wars of the church and of their lord.

were victims or bystanders. In the words of [French scholar] Georges Duby, "Moral obligations and the persuasion of their peers were all that could impose a limit to [the knights'] violence and greed."[87]

It was not until after "the Church laid on the knight the duty of defending the weak, the widow and the orphan, and instructed him that women of noble birth should be especially under his care"[88] that the knight took on the persona that made him an instrument of God's will and the stuff of grand and glorious legend.

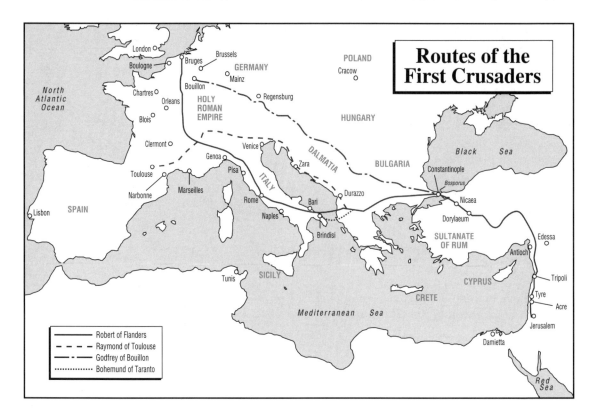

Routes of the First Crusaders

Robert of Flanders
Raymond of Toulouse
Godfrey of Bouillon
Bohemund of Taranto

Beginning in 969 and extending into the middle of the next century, church movements developed the Peace and Truce of God with the intent of limiting warfare within Christendom. The Peace of God decreed "the immunity of the clergy and poor from violence and exploitation,"[89] whereas the Truce of God called for "a suspension of private warfare . . . on certain days or for certain seasons such as Advent and Lent."[90]

In 1054, a church council in Narbonne expanded the terms of the Truce of God, proclaiming: "Let no Christian kill another Christian, for there is no doubt that he who kills a Christian spills the blood of Christ."[91] This meant that a knight had to restrict the practice of his profession of arms to the enemies of Christ. Four decades later, the church obligingly provided him with a plentiful supply of enemies.

In 1095, the church called upon the knights to mount a crusade against the infidels of Islam, ushering in the Age of Chivalry and giving birth to a new breed of knight. (Previously, the knight had earned his keep mostly in the local defense of his lord's realm.)

"Warfare was endemic in medieval society," declares James Harpur. "Chronic rivalries and petty feuds between local princes, lords, and towns were common."[92] But for the next two centuries, the call to defend the Cross would beckon knights and countless other men of arms to work thousands of miles from their homelands.

Commencing in 1097, the Christian powers of Europe, united in their religious fervor, launched the Crusades—eight major military campaigns in the Middle East that attempted to wrest control of the Holy Land from the Muslim nonbelievers. Of the eight numbered

The Battle of Crécy

Perhaps the first truly significant battle of the Hundred Years' War was the Battle of Crécy, in which the forces of England's King Edward III opposed those of France's King Philip VI. In this important confrontation, the foot soldier regained predominance on the battlefield. In the following passage extracted from Elizabeth Hallam's Chronicles of the Age of Chivalry, *fourteenth-century scribe Geoffrey le Baker recounts the action.*

"Towards sunset, after the soldiers had spent the whole day intimidating each other with war-like displays, the battle began, to the sound of trumpets, drums and pipes making a great racket, while shouts of the French almost deafened the English.

It was the French crossbowmen who took the initiative, but their bolts hit none of the English, falling far short of them. The English archers, roused by the great noise of the crossbows, showered their opponents with arrows and put an end to the storm of crossbow bolts with a hail of arrows. . . .

Loud screams arose from the French crossbowmen trampled by the great horses, and from the knights' chargers who had been wounded by arrows, while the French ranks were thrown into fur-ther confusion by the stumbling of the horses [into trenches predug by the English]. Many men fell as they fought with the English, wounded by axes, lances or sword, while many who had suffered no honorable war wound were simply crushed to death in the midst of their own numerous army.

In the heart of this ferocious battle, the noble-spirited Edward of Woodstock, King Edward III's oldest son [the so-called Black Prince], who was at that time sixteen years old, was showing the French his admirable bravery at the head of his division. He stabbed horses, killed knights, struck helmets, snapped lances, craftily parried blows, aided his men, defended himself, helped up his fallen comrades, and encouraged all to good deed by his own example. Nor did he cease from his noble efforts, until the enemy retired behind the mound of their dead. . . .

More than four thousand French knights and nobles died in the battle of Crécy."

The English emerged as victors after two days of fierce fighting, due largely to their use of stronger positions, better discipline, and more firepower.

French knights charge the enemy during the Battle of Crécy.

(major) Crusades, only the First Crusade is generally considered to have been successful: It ended with the capture of Jerusalem and the establishment of four crusader states in the Holy Land. However, the Muslims ultimately reclaimed Jerusalem and drove the crusaders from the Holy Land. The Crusades ended with the fall of Acre, the last Christian bastion in the Middle East, in 1291.

Two more long-lasting campaigns of major stature began in the middle of the following century; namely, the Hundred Years' War between France and England (1337–1457) and the epic confrontation between the Byzantine Empire and the Ottoman Turks (1350–1453).

The Norman Conquest of England led by Duke William of Normandy in 1066 and the War of the Roses from 1452 to 1487—the English civil war between the opposing houses of the Lancasters and the Yorks—represent two additional notable wars in which knights dominated on the battlefield. But knighthood's flower withered and died soon after the introduction of artillery and gunpowder in warfare. Cannons also rendered castles vulnerable and therefore obsolete as defensive bastions. Human ingenuity was continually working to develop new and better ways to kill people.

The Fourth Horseman

During the medieval millennium, famine, plague, and mortal combat combined to lay waste to the land and kill off quite possibly half the population of those one thousand years. Symbolically, the fourth horseman had thundered across Europe leaving death and devastation in his wake. Many Europeans must have more than a time or two recalled the biblical prophecy revealed to John:

> Behold a pale horse: and his name that sat on him was Death, and Hell followed with him. And authority was given to them over a fourth of the earth, to kill with sword and with famine and with pestilence and by the wild beasts of the earth. (Revelation 6:8)

If in their various times the God-fearing folk of medieval Europe felt convinced that they were witnessing the beginning of the end of the world, who, in light of their travails, can fault their misperceptions? Yet, in spite of such despair and depredation, the human spirit endures all manner of malevolent forces and prevails over most, as clearly evidenced by the advanced relics of medieval culture.

6 The Advance of Culture

The cultural heritage of the Middle Ages remains keenly apparent today, embodied in its contributions to architecture and other art, education, the sciences, and technology. "The Middle Ages have left behind a legacy of magnificent buildings and fine art treasures," notes historian John Guy. "The technological advances made in building techniques are unsurpassed, as witnessed by the fact that so many houses, churches and castles have survived."[93]

Citizens of the so-called Dark Ages and beyond were not as rapt in ignorance and incompetence or as shielded from the light of intellect and inventiveness as was later insinuated by many of their successors during the Renaissance. "The illustrated manuscripts, jewelry, pottery, metalwork, sculpture and

An illustration from an illuminated manuscript depicts a scene during the Hundred Years' War. Such illustrations, with their elaborate and amazing miniature detail, are still appreciated as fine works of art.

carved woodwork are just some of the many treasures from the period," offers Guy as a representation of medieval accomplishments. "It was an age astonishing for the richness, beauty and variety of its art, an aspect of medieval life too easily overlooked."[94]

Other significant advances were made in broadly diverse fields during the sixth through tenth centuries: in agriculture (for example, tenant farming and the harnessing of horse to plow), in cloth making, in iron working, in shipbuilding and navigation, and in the service of science/philosophy/religion, which were interconnected. Not the least of these advances came as a result of the ever-increasing need for more churches occasioned by the rise of Christianity.

Architecture

"Every great work of architecture is a cultural symbol," declares historian David Hackett Fischer. "Chartres [Cathedral] was a case in point."[95] In the aftermath of a series of disasters—in which the cathedral was destroyed by enemies and fires—the people of Chartres, France, rebuilt their cathedral seven times. During the twelfth century, nobles and commoners alike twice banded together to haul stone for rebuilding the church in what history has since labeled the Cult of the Carts.

According to Fischer, one early chronicler wrote, "At Chartres, men began with their own shoulders to drag wagons loaded with

The medieval Chartres Cathedral remains a significant architectural accomplishment.

For the nobles and peasants of western Europe, the church provided a spiritual framework for everyday life. It also held out the promise of a life beyond the grave—a hope dramatically rendered in stone in the form of churches and cathedrals whose soaring spires lifted the heart and spirit toward heaven and whose interiors revealed a sacred world of color and wonder.[97]

Two styles of architecture were prevalent during the Middle Ages: the outgoing Romanesque style, which reached the peak of its perfection in the twelfth century, and its successor, the Gothic style. "The massive horizontality of Romanesque architecture would seem to express the submission to God of a society barely emerging from a long slumber," suggests historian Robert S. Lopez. "The light verticality of Gothic architecture would reflect the soaring flight towards God of a society more sure of itself."[98]

Irrespective of style, the church and the castle dominated medieval architecture. Writes historian Norman Davies:

> The late medieval church style, which the nineteenth century was to dub "Gothic," is widely thought to be essentially aesthetic in inspiration—soaring, as it were, towards Heaven. As such, it is often contrasted with the military functionalism of the turrets, barbicans [fortified outer watchtowers], and machicolations [floor openings in overhanging sentry walks used for dropping flaming or heavy missiles on an enemy below] of the castles. In fact, all the main Gothic features, from the pointed arch to the flying buttress, are no less functional than aesthetic; they were devised for the purposes of efficient vaulting and of large window spaces.[99]

stone, wood, grain and other materials to the workshop of the church, whose towers were then rising. . . . One might observe women as well as men dragging [carts] through deep swamps on their knees, beating themselves with whips."[96] The seventh rebuilt cathedral of Chartres still stands in commemoration of their selfless spirit.

Today's student of times past might ask what motivated the people of Chartres to such punishing purpose. One explanation can be found in this commentary by James Harpur:

Gothic architecture prevailed in churches constructed across Latin Christendom, while churches built in the Orthodox Christian East held fast to the Byzantine-influenced Romanesque tradition. "Newfound civic pride gave rise to magnificent belfries, city halls, and cloth halls," adds Davies. "Fine [Gothic] examples were built at Brussels (1402), Arras, Ghent, Ypres (1302), and Cracow (1392)."[100]

Elegant civic structures reflected the new affluence and political power of an emerging bourgeoisie. But as historian Peter Draper points out, "The scale and pretension of the architecture of churches can be equally expressive of political power as of religious aspiration." The towering Gothic spires of Christianity stood as ever-present reminders of the church's dominant role in medieval society. "To make the most of the evidence which these buildings can afford," avers Draper, "we need to interpret the architecture in a variety of ways and, above all, to keep in mind the vital relationship between architecture and the other arts."[101]

The Other Arts

"Art for art's sake was a concept that was totally alien to the medieval mind," contends James Harpur. "Artistic endeavor was the handmaiden of its mistress, the church, and had the function of teaching points of theology, morals, and discipline and elevating the mind."[102] In the beginning, to be sure, medieval art focused on religious themes and was centered and developed in the church. Norman Davies concurs:

> Most medieval arts developed in the setting of church or cathedral. Painting was directed either to icons and altar-pieces or to the religious scenes of church mu-

rals. Book illumination was undertaken to adorn bibles and psalters [collections of psalms]. Sculpture in stone gloried in the statues and tableaux of cathedral fronts, and in the effigies of tombs and chantries [chapels]. Sculpture in wood embellished choir stalls or choir screens. Stained glass filled the vast expanses of Gothic church windows. "All art was more or less applied art."[103]

But all art was not inspired by or related to the church. As medieval society grew more affluent, evidences of secular art, never without some representation, increased. The wealthy middle class followed the lead of princes and started commissioning their portraits or sculptured images. Artists outside the clergy began applying their talents to the art

An illustration from the Book of Kells *depicts the Virgin Mary with the Christ child. Most medieval art portrayed religious themes.*

of illumination, that is, the art of decorating (or illuminating) with gold or silver (or other bright colors) or with intricate designs or miniature illustrations. The art was applied principally to book manuscripts, such as the popular *chansons de geste* (epic poems) and the fashionable books of hours (prayer books). Illuminated herbaries, books describing the medicinal and culinary uses of herbs, and bestiaries, tomes depicting real or imaginary animals, also became favorite outlets for the arts.

To illuminate a book, of course, it first had to be written. The literate class of thirteenth-century England regarded French as the language of elegant conversation; those who did not speak it were held in low esteem. Many books of that period were written in French. Because French is one of the several Romance languages stemming from Latin, a book written in French was called a *romance*. In a narrower sense, the term is applied to a specific kind of literature: in medieval times, to a tale based on legend, chivalric love, and adventure or the supernatural, and more currently, to a love story.

In its original sense, the romance, with its characteristic emphasis on individuals rather than groups, became highly popular among nobles and knights. With regard to this "literature of aspiration," in which "the feelings and aspirations of the main characters are keenly analyzed," Elizabeth Hallam's *Chronicles of the Age of Chivalry* comments on the genre's popular appeal:

> Works which described a life of rags to riches appealed to the knightly class, as did tales of King Arthur's court, where the legendary Round Table blurred discrepancies of wealth and status. In this literary world, a country knight could easily imagine that he was the social equal of a great earl.

The most influential work of the 13th century was, however, a continuation of the *Roman de la Rose* [an unfinished poetic allegory epitomizing courtly love]. Written in about 1270 by Jean de Meung, it reflects a very different and at times satirical attitude to religion and the world. The outdated conventions of courtly love which were so strongly emphasized in the first part of the romance are rejected and, instead, nature is celebrated. . . .

Jean de Meung believed that nature was the work of God and was in conformity with His will, and that it had designed sexual intercourse for the propagation of the species. He believed that the created world was good and that happiness was possible and desirable on this side of heaven. The rose became the symbol of the victory of God, nature and mankind over death.[104]

Music

Unlike the finely conceived and crafted illuminated books and the enduring opulence of medieval architecture and other visual art forms, much of the music of medieval muses failed to reach the ears of posterity.

Because musicians and minstrels improvised or sang and played their music from memory for hundreds of years, and because many of them were illiterate, much of the music outside the church was not written down and did not survive the ages. Some sources estimate that the words and music of only about thirty nonclerical English and Anglo-French songs composed between 1177 and 1377 have carried over to modern times.

"Unfortunately for modern researchers, most songs were never written down," affirms

Those Who Pursue Great Riches

In the second part of the thirteenth-century French poetic allegory Romance of the Rose, *Jean de Meung (or Jeun de Meun) severely criticizes a society that he perceives as corrupt. The following extract from the allegory is taken, in part, from Norman Cantor's* The Medieval Reader.

"And it remains true, no matter whom the idea displeases, that no merchant lives at ease. He has put his heart into such a state of war that he burns alive to acquire more, nor will he ever have acquired enough. He fears to lose the wealth that he has gained, and he pursues the remainder that he will never see himself possess, for his strongest desire is to acquire another's property. He has undertaken a wondrous task: he aspires to drink up the whole Seine, but he will never be able to drink so much that there will not remain more. This is the distress, the fire, the anguish which lasts forever; it is the pain, the battle which tears his guts and torments him in his lack: the more he acquires, the more he needs.

Lawyers and physicians are all shackled by this bond. They sell knowledge for pennies; they all hang themselves by this rope. They find gain so sweet and pleasant that the physician wishes he had sixty patients for the one he has, and the lawyer thirty cases for one, indeed two hundred or two thousand, so much covetousness and guile burn in their hearts.

The same is true of the divines who walk the earth: when they preach in order to acquire honors, favors, or riches, they acquire, in addition, hearts torn by anguish. They do not live lawfully. But, above all, those who pursue vainglory buy their soul's death. Such a deceiver is himself deceived, for you know that however much a preacher profits others, he profits himself nothing: for good preaching that comes in fact from evil intention is worth nothing to the preacher, even though it may save others. . . . Three great misfortunes come to those who lead such lives: first, they acquire riches through great labor; then, as long as they do not cease guarding their treasures, fear keeps them in great distress; and, in the end, they grieve to leave their wealth. Those who pursue great riches die and live in this torment."

---

historian Sherrilyn Kenyon, "and since the first musical staff didn't appear until the late twelfth century, what little we have exists without the accompanying instrumental chords."[105] Beginning late in the fourteenth century, however, musical patronage that had centered earlier in the monasteries and churches now shifted to the courts of royalty. Music slipped the bonds of religious constraints and took on a more worldly appeal.

Composers, no longer fearful of offending religious sensibilities, began documenting their music and claiming ownership.

In sum, most medieval art imitated life, which centered on the church throughout most of the Middle Ages. "Art had the task of embellishing the forms in which life was lived with beauty," writes Dutch historian Johan Huizinga. "What was sought was not art itself, but the beautiful life."[106]

Medieval street musicians entertain passersby. Because medieval music was frequently improvised or performed from memory, little of it survives in written form.

Therefore, according to Huizinga, art for its own sake did not find expression—except possibly subconsciously in the mind of its creator—until much later. It is likely that improved educational resources vastly aided creative minds to find outlets for their creativity.

Education

The rise of Europe's first universities accompanied the growth of towns in the thirteenth century. Towns became centers of learning and education. Universities flourished under the burgeoning wealth of a new mercantile economy and new exposure to classical learning through trade contact with the Byzantine East.

Bernard, chancellor of Chartres Cathedral, intentionally or not, set the tone for the medieval attitude toward learning. In contrasting scholars of his own period with those of the classical age, he observed: "We are dwarfs mounted on the shoulders of giants, so that we can see more and farther than they."[107] Prior to the rise of universities, monastic and cathedral schools provided most of the education available in the twelfth and thirteenth centuries.

Beginning in the eleventh century, the great cathedral schools of France and England—for example, in Chartres, Reims, Paris, Orléans, York, and Lincoln—moved into prominence as centers of learning. Medieval intellectuals called *scholastics* took the lead in this renewed interest in learning. Historian Joseph Dahmus explains:

> The term "scholastic" is applied to this new scholar of the eleventh century who turned with special interest to the study of dialectic [logic]. In its simplest application, the designation "scholastic" might be given to any scholar or schoolman. As the term came to be applied, it referred more specifically to the scholar who pursued the study of logic and of metaphysics [a branch of philosophy concerned with the fundamental nature of reality] in his conviction that a knowledge of those subjects would facilitate his study of Christian theology. Scholasticism might therefore be

defined as the system of thought that dominated the schools of the Middle Ages from the eleventh to the fifteenth century, which had as its objective the clarification of Christian faith with the help of reason.[108]

The basic premise of scholasticism, according to Dahmus, held that "faith and reason complemented one another and that reason was useful in explaining the faith."[109] This premise was embraced and expanded by such notable thinkers as French philosopher Peter Abelard (1079–1142), Italian theologian St. Thomas Aquinas (1225–1274), Franciscan scholar St. Bonaventure (1221–1274), and Scottish philosopher Duns Scotus (1265–1308).

Scholasticism began to decline when its premise came under attack by William of Ockham (1285–1349). He argued that man can accept the existence of God only through faith and revelation. God, he insisted, does not work through reason; God's power is absolute and illimitable. He does good because it pleases him to do so, not, as Thomas Aquinas believed, because God is beneficent by nature. Ockham's controversial opinions caused a reordering of scholastic thought. Scholarly thinking shifted away from God and "swung to man, to grace, free will, and sanctification."[110]

"Meantime as scholasticism rose and flowered," continues Joseph Dahmus, "it witnessed, if it did not give birth to, another intellectual development. That was the medieval university." He describes its origin and interests this way:

Both in origin and in interests, the university was so closely associated with scholasticism that it is impossible to separate the one from the other. What happened in substance was this, that as scholasticism grew more popular, its interests broader,

and the new knowledge from the Islamic and Byzantine worlds permitted a vast expansion of its subject matter, the traditional cathedral school underwent a transformation: it became a university. This, then, was one of the major factors in the rise of the university, namely, the vigorous intellectual life of the cathedral schools of the twelfth century.[111]

It bears mentioning at this point that crusaders returning from military expeditions in the Holy Land bore with them much of "the new knowledge from the Islamic and Byzantine worlds" for some two hundred years, an enabling factor in Dahmus's conclusion:

The other principal factor was the higher learning that came to the West by way of Islam and Constantinople and which the scholars seized upon and sought to assimilate. This learning includes the works of Aristotle, Ptolemy, and Galen, in addition [to] the commentaries of Arabic and Jewish scholars, and the *Corpus Juris Civilis* of Justinian. From the interaction of these two factors, the intellectual vigor of scholasticism with this higher learning from the East, sprang the medieval university.[112]

A typical curriculum at a medieval university was based on the seven liberal arts: grammar, dialogue, rhetoric, music, arithmetic, geometry, and astronomy. The universities at Chartres and Laon in northern France, and in Paris, ranked among the more important early learning institutions. Two-time Pulitzer Prize–winning historian Barbara W. Tuchman comments:

Though Oxford was growing as a center of intellectual interest, the University of

Paris was still the theological arbiter of Europe, and the libraries of its separate faculties, some numbering up to a thousand volumes, augmented its glory. Added to these were the fine library of Notre Dame and no less than 28 booksellers, not counting open-air bookstalls. Here were "abundant orchards of all manner of books," wrote an enraptured English visitor; "what a mighty stream of pleasure made glad our hearts when we visited Paris, the paradise of the world."

Despite the English visitor's ebullience, not all in thirteenth-century Paris warranted praise on high. Notes Tuchman:

As a capital city with a great university, Paris was host to a turbulent horde of students from all over Europe. They had privileged status not subject to local justice but only to the King, with the result that their crimes and disorders went largely unpunished. They lived miserably,

In a fifteenth-century illustration, a professor lectures to students at the University of Paris. The first universities were founded during the Middle Ages.

overcharged for dirty rooms in dark neighborhoods. They sat on stools in cold lecture halls lit only by two candles and were perennially complained of for debauchery, rape, robbery, and "all other enormities hateful to God."[113]

On a higher plane, the rise of the medieval university led to a proliferation of professional people, intent on delving into the secrets of the sciences as they were then known to exist.

The Sciences

The English word *science* derives from the Latin word *scientia*, which means "knowing" or "being skilled." Today, the sciences are generally classified into three categories: *physical* sciences—physics, mathematics, chemistry, astronomy, and earth sciences; *life* sciences—biology and medicine; and *social* sciences—economics, sociology, geography, political science, and cultural anthropology. "Law, the discipline concerned with the customs and rules governing a community," according to *Compton's Interactive Encyclopedia*, "is also sometimes regarded as a science, particularly comparative law." But in medieval times, "the branches of study that are now called sciences . . . fell under the heading of philosophy, an umbrella term that suggested the pursuit of knowledge."[114]

Other opinions on the state of medieval science cast some doubt as to the integrity of knowledge that was being pursued under the "scientific umbrella." For instance, Robert Lopez writes: "Science, it has been claimed, was born of a marriage of mathematics and magic. Without the drive of irrational impulses, illusion, imagination, it would be hard for scholarship to climb out of the old rut."[115]

Moreover, according to Norman Davies, medieval science "was inextricably bound up with theology. There was no clear sense of the separation of physical and spiritual phenomena, so that exploring the 'secrets of nature' was frequently seen as immodest prying 'into the womb of Mother Church.'"[116]

Historians largely agree that the scientific achievements of the Middle Ages were slight. Reasons for the dearth of scientific gains abounded. In the medieval West, science and philosophy matured amid the chaos and fear of an age replete with myth and legend, demons and divination, astrology and sorcery, miracle and magic, omens and soothsayers, and a multitude of detracting and often frightening superstitions. Moreover, the dark vestiges of European paganism continued to cast shadows on scientific efforts to illuminate the intellect.

Writes Will Durant:

A multitude of mysterious and supernatural beings had descended into Christianity from pagan antiquity, and were still coming in from Germany, Scandinavia, and Ireland as trolls, elves, giants, fairies, goblins, gnomes, ogres, banshees, mysterious dragons, blood-sucking vampires, and new superstitions were always entering Europe from the East.[117]

In spite of vehement denunciation by the church, black magic (calling on demons to gain control over events) was practiced clandestinely across the land, as was witchcraft, which never lacked for want of believers. Some religious scholars think that the church formulated certain prayers and exorcising ceremonies as psychological balm for soothing superstitious minds.

Even the practice of medieval medicine might be considered to some degree an extension of theology and its attendant ritual.

Students attend a class in philosophy. Such courses were often tainted with misconceptions, including myth, superstition, and magic.

One notable theologian, St. Augustine, bishop of Hippo, attributed the diseases of humankind to demons, and another, Martin Luther, agreed with his predecessor's conclusions. It therefore followed logically that the antidote for diseases lay in prayer or some form of religious rite of procession.

Understandably, then, medieval scientific accomplishments were few, and, as Norman Davies puts it, "most of the landmark achievements came from the work of scattered individuals."[118]

Roger Bacon's mid–thirteenth century experiments with optics and machines, for example, resulted from his determination to expose corruption and lay bare the fallacies of superstition. He eventually gained a reputation for diverse and unconventional expertise in philosophy, alchemy, and magic. Pierre de Maricourt (Peter the Stranger), Bacon's mentor, developed a benchmark thesis on magnetism in 1269.

The Silesian Witello, or Vitellon (1230–1280), drew acclaim for his elemental discourse on optics. In his work he separated the eye's mechanical operation from the mind's coordinating function, which some scholars think cleared the way for today's psychology.

Nicole Oresme (1320–1382), French cleric, mathematician, philosopher, and later the bishop of Lisieux, earned recognition for his deliberations on the economics of money, his work in astronomy, and his opposition to astrology.

Although the gains of medieval scientists were modest at best, would-be latter-day critics would do well to consider Will Durant's plea for moderation: "If the achievements of medieval science in the West should seem meager . . . let us remember that it grew in a hostile environment of superstition and magic, in an age that drew the best minds into law and theology, and at a time when nearly all men believed that the major problems of cosmic and human origin, nature, and destiny had been solved."[119]

The practice of law, enhanced by some of the "best minds" of the time, stands at the forefront of medieval professional achievement. "The legal profession became thoroughly professionalized," notes historian Norman F. Cantor, "and English common law assumed the organizational form and behavior patterns that still exist in the United States and Canada, as well as in Britain, for better or worse." By contrast, Cantor writes less glowingly about the practice of medicine:

Physicians and surgeons made no progress in their professional standing or in improving their contribution to society. Instead they did a lot of damage. Panicked by the Black Death, whose cause mystified them, they convinced Europeans to close their windows and sheath them with heavy drapes to keep out the "bad air" that, they alleged, brought plague and to

Roger Bacon tried to purge the fallacies of superstition by using provable experiments to develop his theories on optics and machines.

stop taking baths, which, they claimed, opened the pores to the dread disease. This quack medicine was not completely revised until the twentieth century.[120]

Although scientific achievements of the medieval millennium lagged, overall, behind those of earlier and later cultures, the medieval mind did not lack ingenuity. The destiny of medieval souls was resolved largely by the inventiveness of medieval minds, which gave rise to the advance of technology.

Invention and Technology

Necessity, as it so often does, led to numerous key inventions, which, in turn, spurred the development of technology. According to historians Joseph and Frances Gies, "the innovative technology of the Middle Ages" was once thought to be the product of "unknown geniuses who worked in isolation, surrounded by a sea of darkness." But today, say the Gieses, it appears as "the silent contribution of many hands and minds working together."[121]

As the Gieses explain, the greatest changes did not occur in the form of any particular individual invention but as slow unnoticed revolts against the existing ways of doing things. Such gradual changes were found "in agriculture, in wind and water power, in building construction, in textile manufacturing, in communications, in metallurgy, in weaponry— taking place in incremental improvements, large or small, in tools, techniques, and the organization of work."[122]

Many of today's historians view these technological advances as an almost continual social process rather than an unrelated succession of single actions. Such thinking forms a part of a new, broader change in historical theory that views the technological innovations of *all* ages this way. But no matter how history is viewed today, there remains little doubt that, as the Gieses phrase it, "one of the great technological revolutions took place during the medieval millennium with the disappearance of mass slavery, the shift to water-and wind-power, the introduction of the open-field system of agriculture, and the importation, adaptation, or invention of an array of devices, from the wheelbarrow to double-entry bookkeeping, climaxed by those two avatars [manifestations] of modern Western civilization, firearms and printing."[123]

In concluding their remarkable study of invention and technology in the Middle Ages, the Gieses write:

> The Middle Ages used [technology] sometimes wisely, sometimes recklessly, often for dubious purposes, seldom with a thought for the future, and with only a dim awareness of the scientific and mathematical laws governing it. But operating on instinct, insight, trial and error, and perseverance, the craftsmen and craftswomen, the entrepreneurs, the working monks and the clerical intellectuals, and the artist-engineers all transformed the world, on balance very much to the world's advantage.[124]

The same might be said of countless others who contributed to the often struggling but doggedly persistent advance of culture in the Middle Ages. Acknowledgment and gratitude to them all.

Over Distant Horizons

The advance of medieval culture marched out of the Dark Ages and into a re-awakening of intellectualism that commenced at about 1500. In its one-thousand-year journey through time, the culture of the Middle Ages compiled an impressive legacy that is too often overlooked or underrated.

"We are tempted to think of the Middle Ages as a fallow interval between the fall of the Roman Empire in the West (476) and the discovery of America," writes Will Durant. But, as he reminds his readers, "the boundary between 'medieval' and 'modern' is always advancing; and our age of coal and oil and sooty slums may some day be accounted medieval by an era of cleaner power and more gracious life."[125]

Lest modern-day students of times past adopt the superior air of Renaissance critics in their assessment of the medieval age, they would do well to ponder at length on the words of that gentle historian. To aid today's student to reflect without bias on medieval matters, a summary look at the "hard-won wealth of our medieval heritage"[126] might prove advantageous.

Our Medieval Heritage

"Because of the disorder of the period 1300–1500," writes Norman Cantor, "those who admire the medieval heritage and seek some kind of revival of medievalism in our time look to the earlier centuries from St. Augus-tine and St. Benedict to St. Bernard of Clairvaux and St. Thomas Aquinas for inspiration, contrasted with the materialism and decadence of the closing years of the twentieth century."[127] Professor Cantor's description of the would-be revivalist's visions of medieval times represents, by itself, a fair summation of our medieval heritage.

According to Cantor, the revivalist envisioned life in the Middle Ages as a life unregulated by the strict control of a central government bureaucracy; a life, therefore, in which people were left to decide for themselves what was best for them and their society. They saw "a culture that arose out of chaos, violence, and cruelty by the application of learned intelligence to social behavior" and "a world that recognized the capacity of individuals to love God and human beings and turned this love into wonderful artistic and literary expressions."[128]

In his mind's eye, the revivalist viewed the medieval world as one that combined reason and tradition to create prospering, stable communities in harmony with their environment. To the revivalist, the "religious devotion and moral commitment" of medieval times "that led also to the founding of great universities and the support of learning, art, and imaginative literature"[129] represented a model for living.

In his description, Cantor recognizes, of course, that the medieval world was not without imperfections:

Life expectancy was short, and disease was incontestable. It was a world burdened by royal authority and social hierarchy inherited from ancient times. Its piety and devotion were affected by fanaticism and a potential for persecution. Its intellectuals were given to too abstract and not enough practical thinking. But it exhibited as elevated a culture, as peaceful a community, as benign a political system, as high-minded and popular a faith as the world has ever seen.[130]

Fellow historian Joseph Dahmus bears witness to Professor Cantor's vision of our medieval heritage: "By 1500 when time ran

The Honor of the Order of Chivalry

To this day, the romantic image of the chivalrous knight, bedecked in armor and astride a great charger, remains the enduring symbol of the Middle Ages. In the conclusion of William Caxton's translation of The Book of the Ordre of Chyvalry *(1484)— reprinted in* The Knight in History *by Frances Gies—latter-day knights are implored to leave their vices behind and revisit the deeds of their predecessors.*

"OH YE KNIGHTS OF ENGLAND, WHERE IS THE CUSTOM AND USAGE OF NOBLE CHIVALRY THAT WAS USED IN THE DAYS OF KING ARTHUR? WHAT DO YE NOW BUT GO TO THE BAGNIOS [BROTHELS] AND PLAY AT DICE. . . . LEAVE THIS, LEAVE IT AND READ THE NOBLE VOLUMES OF THE HOLY GRAIL, OF LAUNCELOT, OF GALAHAD, OF TRISTAM, OF PERSEFOREST, OF PERCIVAL, OF GAWAIN, AND MANY MORE. THERE SHALL YE SEE MANHOOD, COURTESY, AND GENTLENESS. AND LOOK IN LATER DAYS OF THE NOBLE ACTS SINCE THE CONQUEST. . . . READ FROISSART, AND ALSO BEHOLD THAT VICTORIOUS AND NOBLE KING HARRY THE FIFTH, AND THE CAPTAINS UNDER HIM . . . AND MANY OTHERS WHOSE NAMES SHINE GLORIOUSLY BY THEIR VIRTUOUS NOBLESSE AND ACTS THAT THEY DID IN HONOR OF THE ORDER OF CHIVALRY."

An eleventh-century illustration depicts the epitome of chivalry, Sir Lancelot, with the object of his affection, Queen Guinevere.

out for the Middle Ages, Western Europe had attained in its universities, literature, art, learning, science, technology, expanding capitalism, and governmental institutions a level of cultural, political, and economic maturity no other part of the world, whether Islamic or Oriental, could match."[131]

A New Era Opens

Many of the "unmatchable attainments" of medieval societies helped to sway the course of history, perhaps none more so than the church's recognition of the intrinsic worth of the individual. As John H. Mundy, professor of history at Columbia University, phrases it, "All who lived well and faithfully were as good in God's eyes as the religious. . . . The day had begun when the good man, whatever his earthly vocation, could be a monk in his inner calling."[132]

In the emerging world of the later Middle Ages, the good man for the first time stood on equal footing with priests, prophets, princes, and kings, his worth no longer measured by social ranking but by how well he performed in his chosen field. This monumental change in social attitudes represents possibly the most important step taken by medieval society along the path to today's world, as Professor Mundy explains:

It is perhaps this unification of the practical and spiritual in the soul of each man, itself the very essence of later secularism, that is the greatest legacy of the later Middle Ages. That it had "advantages," there is no doubt. Without the spiritual liberation of the professions of learning, knowledge would still be impeded by external and ecclesiastical restraints. Without the loosing of the soldier's profession from ec-

clesiastical inhibitions, Europe's culture would not have conquered the world.[133]

Perhaps equally important to European growth and expansion were the political changes that occurred across Europe in the mid- and late fifteenth century. On the Iberian Peninsula, Spain united in 1479 as a result of the marriage of Ferdinand II of Aragon and Isabella of Castile. In 1492, Spain conquered Granada, the last Moorish (Muslim) kingdom.

North of Spain, England and France, and their allies, after twelve decades of fighting,

No Fear

The irrepressible spirit of the Middle Ages that carried over to the Renaissance and emboldened the voyages of discovery is perhaps no better expressed than in the words of Jean de Beuil, a fifteenth-century knight. His thoughts on war and facing death are excerpted from Barbara Tuchman's A Distant Mirror.

"How seductive is war! When you know your quarrel to be just and your blood ready for combat, tears come to your eyes. The heart feels a sweet loyalty and pity to see one's friend expose his body in order to do and accomplish the command of the Creator. Alongside him, one prepares to live or die. From that comes a delectable sense which no one who has not experienced it will never know how to explain. Do you think that a man who has experienced that can fear death? Never, for he is so comforted, so enraptured that he knows not where he is and truly fears nothing."

Christopher Columbus lands in the New World. Columbus's voyages, at the end of the Middle Ages, launched the Age of Discovery.

finally settled their differences and ended the Hundred Years' War. The French then realigned their foreign policy and diverted a substantial military force to Italy, where they introduced new weapons and tactics in their subsequent campaigns and changed the face of warfare. These events triggered a resurgence of political and economic growth in the Mediterranean world. But as the Middle Ages drew to a close, an event was taking shape that would ultimately carry far greater significance for most Europeans—an event that would cause them to look beyond the seas.

In 1492, Christopher Columbus (Christoforo Colombo)—backed by Ferdinand and Isabella of Spain, who wanted to add wealth and new territories to their domain—sailed across the Atlantic Ocean to the Caribbean Sea. In that voyage, and in three later voyages (1493–1504), Columbus discovered most of the islands in the area and sailed as far west as the coast of Central America. His voyages opened the door to the New World and to the Age of Discovery, and changed the world forever. A bounty of intrepid seafarers and explorers followed in his wake.

At the start of the sixteenth century, the rulers of Europe launched additional voyages of discovery, and the irrepressible spirit of the Middle Ages carried into the next human age. More important, ordinary men and women began envisioning their futures beyond the confines of Europe. And the day drew ever nearer when many among them would sail over distant horizons and act out their lives in adventures beyond their wildest dreams.

Notes

Introduction: A Thousand Years of Transition

1. Robert S. Lopez, *The Birth of Europe*. New York: M. Evans, 1967, p. 30.
2. Lopez, *The Birth of Europe*, p. 30.
3. Judy Jones and William Wilson, *An Incomplete Education*. New York: Ballantine Books, 1987, pp. 567–68.
4. Norman F. Cantor, *The Civilization of the Middle Ages*. New York: HarperCollins, 1993, pp. 1, 5.
5. Will Durant, *The Age of Faith: A History of Medieval Civilization—Christian, Islamic, and Judaic—from Constantine to Dante: A.D. 325–1300*, vol. 4 of *The Story of Civilization*. New York: Simon and Schuster, 1950, p. 43.
6. "The Middle Ages," in *Compton's Interactive Encyclopedia*, Version 3.00. Compton's New Media, copyright © 1994, 1995.
7. James Harpur, with Elizabeth Hallam, consultant, *Revelations: The Medieval World*. New York: Henry Holt, 1995, p. 10.
8. Quoted in Harpur, *Revelations*, p. 10.
9. Quoted in Julius Kirshner and Karl F. Morrison, eds., *Medieval Europe*, vol. 4 of *Readings in Western Civilization*. Chicago: University of Chicago Press, 1986, p. 56.

Chapter 1: The Medieval Social Order

10. Durant, *The Age of Faith*, p. 553.
11. Ebenezer Cobham Brewer, *Dictionary of Phrase and Fable*, 14th ed., ed. Ivor H. Evans. New York: Harper & Row, 1989, p. 417.

12. Norman Davies, *Europe: A History*. New York: Oxford University Press, 1996, p. 311.
13. Davies, *Europe*, p. 312.
14. Madeleine Pelner Cosman, *Medieval Wordbook*. New York: Facts On File, 1996, p. 51.
15. Davies, *Europe*, p. 314.
16. Norman F. Cantor, ed., *The Medieval Reader*. New York: HarperCollins, 1994, p. xiii.
17. Cantor, *The Medieval Reader*, p. xiii.
18. Durant, *The Age of Faith*, p. 646.
19. Cantor, *The Medieval Reader*, p. 3.
20. Cantor, *The Medieval Reader*, pp. 3–4.
21. Sherrilyn Kenyon, *The Writer's Guide to Everyday Life in the Middle Ages: The British Isles from 500 to 1500*. Cincinnati: Writer's Digest Books, 1995, p. 132.
22. Cantor, *The Medieval Reader*, p. 28.
23. Kenyon, *The Writer's Guide to Everyday Life in the Middle Ages*, p. 132.
24. Kenyon, *The Writer's Guide to Everyday Life in the Middle Ages*, p. 132.
25. Harpur, *Revelations*, p. 19.
26. Cantor, *The Medieval Reader*, p. 29.
27. Durant, *The Age of Faith*, p. 646.
28. Cantor, *The Medieval Reader*, p. 61.

Chapter 2: Rural Life

29. Quoted in Frances and Joseph Gies, *Cathedral, Forge, and Waterwheel*. New York: HarperCollins, 1994, p. 59.
30. Joseph and Frances Gies, *Life in a Medieval Castle*. New York: Harper & Row, 1974, pp. 147–48.
31. Joseph Dahmus, *A History of the Middle Ages*. New York: Barnes & Noble Books, 1995, p. 235.

32. Philip Warner, *The Medieval Castle*. New York: Barnes & Noble Books, 1993, pp. 198–99.

33. John Guy, *Medieval Life*. Tunbridge Wells, England: Addax, 1995, p. 8.

34. Kenyon, *The Writer's Guide to Everyday Life in the Middle Ages*, p. 56.

35. Harpur, *Revelations*, p. 28.

36. Quoted in Joseph and Frances Gies, *Life in a Medieval Castle*, pp. 123–24.

37. Guy, *Medieval Life*, p. 14.

38. Guy, *Medieval Life*, p. 15.

39. Harpur, *Revelations*, p. 56.

40. Quoted in Warner, *The Medieval Castle*, p. 202.

Chapter 3: Urban Life

41. Harpur, *Revelations*, p. 42.

42. Harpur, *Revelations*, p. 43.

43. Quoted in "The Middle Ages," *Compton's Interactive Encyclopedia*.

44. Quoted in Elizabeth Hallam, ed., *Chronicles of the Crusades*. Godalming, England: Bramley Books, 1996, p. 72.

45. Durant, *The Age of Faith*, pp. 640–41.

46. Quoted in Joseph and Frances Gies, *Life in a Medieval City*. New York: Harper & Row, 1969, p. 34.

47. Joseph and Frances Gies, *Life in a Medieval City*, p. 34.

48. Joseph and Frances Gies, *Life in a Medieval City*, p. 45.

49. Durant, *The Age of Faith*, p. 642.

50. Quoted in Durant, *The Age of Faith*, p. 642.

51. Cantor, *The Civilization of the Middle Ages*, p. 477.

52. Guy, *Medieval Life*, p. 2.

53. Barbara W. Tuchman, *A Distant Mirror: The Calamitous 14th Century*. New York: Ballantine Books, 1979, p. 157.

54. Tuchman, *A Distant Mirror*, p. 216.

55. Durant, *The Age of Faith*, pp. 640–42.

Chapter 4: Money and the Growth of Trade

56. Quoted in Cantor, *The Medieval Reader*, p. 268.

57. John H. Munro, "Patterns of Trade, Money, and Credit," in Thomas A. Brady Jr., Heiko A. Oberman, and James D. Tracy, eds., *Structures and Assertions*, vol. 1 of *Handbook of European History, 1400–1600: Late Middle Ages, Renaissance, and Reformation*. Grand Rapids, MI: William B. Eerdmans, 1994, p. 147.

58. Lopez, *The Birth of Europe*, p. 296.

59. Durant, *The Age of Faith*, pp. 626–27.

60. Harpur, *Revelations*, p. 58.

61. Dahmus, *A History of the Middle Ages*, p. 265.

62. Harpur, *Revelations*, p. 58.

63. Quoted in Durant, *The Age of Faith*, pp. 627–28.

64. Durant, *The Age of Faith*, p. 628.

65. Quoted in Elizabeth Hallam, ed., *Chronicles of the Age of Chivalry*. London: Tiger Books International, 1995, p. 281.

66. Hallam, *Chronicles of the Age of Chivalry*, p. 281.

67. Durant, *The Age of Faith*, p. 628.

68. Durant, *The Age of Faith*, p. 629.

69. Elizabeth Hallam, ed., *The Plantagenet Encyclopedia: An Alphabetical Guide to 400 Years of English History*. New York: Crescent Books, 1996, p. 89.

70. Kenyon, *The Writer's Guide to Everyday Life in the Middle Ages*, p. 47.

71. Lopez, *The Birth of Europe*, p. 143.

72. Davies, *Europe*, p. 340.

73. Davies, *Europe*, pp. 340–41.

74. Lopez, *The Birth of Europe*, p. 143.

75. Durant, *The Age of Faith*, p. 634.

76. Durant, *The Age of Faith*, p. 637.

77. David Hackett Fischer, *The Great Wave: Price Revolutions and the Rhythm of*

History. New York: Oxford University Press, 1996, pp. 20–21.

78. Fischer, *The Great Wave*, p. 35.

Chapter 5: Famine, Pestilence, War, and Death

79. Fischer, *The Great Wave*, p. 35.
80. Tuchman, *A Distant Mirror*, pp. 24–25.
81. Quoted in Hallam, *Chronicles of the Age of Chivalry*, p. 192.
82. Harpur, *Revelations*, p. 60.
83. Davies, *Europe*, p. 409.
84. Philip Ziegler, *The Black Death*. Phoenix Mill, England: Alan Sutton, 1995, p. 10.
85. Brewer, *Dictionary of Phrase and Fable*, p. 119.
86. Quoted in Frances Gies, *The Knight in History*. New York: Harper & Row, 1987, p. 7.
87. Gies, *The Knight in History*, p. 27.
88. A. V. B. Norman, *The Medieval Soldier*. New York: Barnes & Noble Books, 1993, p. 145.
89. Jonathan Riley-Smith, *The Crusades: A Short History*. New Haven, CT, and London: Yale University Press, 1987, p. 14.
90. Brewer, *Dictionary of Phrase and Fable*, p. 1,124.
91. Quoted in Gies, *The Knight in History*, p. 20.
92. Harpur, *Revelations*, p. 97.

Chapter 6: The Advance of Culture

93. Guy, *Medieval Life*, p. 16.
94. Guy, *Medieval Life*, p. 16.
95. Fischer, *The Great Wave*, p. 12.
96. Quoted in Fischer, *The Great Wave*, p. 12.
97. Harpur, *Revelations*, p. 64.
98. Lopez, *The Birth of Europe*, p. 189.
99. Davies, *Europe*, p. 440.
100. Davies, *Europe*, p. 441.
101. Peter Draper, "The Architectural Set-ting of Gothic Art," in Nigel Saul, ed., *Age of Chivalry: Art and Society in Late Medieval England*. London: Brockhampton Press, 1995, p. 60.
102. Harpur, *Revelations*, p. 66.
103. Davies, *Europe*, p. 441.
104. Hallam, *Chronicles of the Age of Chivalry*, p. 55.
105. Kenyon, *The Writer's Guide to Everyday Life in the Middle Ages*, p. 70.
106. Johan Huizinga, *The Autumn of the Middle Ages*, trans. Rodney J. Payton and Ulrich Mammitzsch. Chicago: University of Chicago Press, 1996, p. 296.
107. Quoted in Harpur, *Revelations*, p. 52.
108. Dahmus, *A History of the Middle Ages*, p. 325.
109. Dahmus, *A History of the Middle Ages*, p. 333.
110. Dahmus, *A History of the Middle Ages*, p. 334.
111. Dahmus, *A History of the Middle Ages*, p. 334.
112. Dahmus, *A History of the Middle Ages*, p. 334.
113. Tuchman, *A Distant Mirror*, pp. 159–60.
114. "The Sciences," in *Compton's Interactive Encyclopedia*.
115. Lopez, *The Birth of Europe*, pp. 367–68.
116. Davies, *Europe*, p. 435.
117. Durant, *The Age of Faith*, p. 984.
118. Davies, *Europe*, pp. 435–36.
119. Durant, *The Age of Faith*, p. 989.
120. Cantor, *The Civilization of the Middle Ages*, p. 564.
121. Frances and Joseph Gies, *Cathedral, Forge, and Waterwheel*, p. 2.
122. Frances and Joseph Gies, *Cathedral, Forge, and Waterwheel*, p. 2.
123. Frances and Joseph Gies, *Cathedral, Forge, and Waterwheel*, p. 15.
124. Frances and Joseph Gies, *Cathedral, Forge, and Waterwheel*, p. 291.

Afterword: Over Distant Horizons

125. Durant, *The Age of Faith*, p. 1,082.
126. Durant, *The Age of Faith*, p. 1,082.
127. Cantor, *The Civilization of the Middle Ages*, p. 565.
128. Cantor, *The Civilization of the Middle Ages*, p. 565.
129. Cantor, *The Civilization of the Middle Ages*, p. 565.
130. Cantor, *The Civilization of the Middle Ages*, p. 565.
131. Dahmus, *A History of the Middle Ages*, p. 393.
132. Quoted in John Garraty and Peter Gay, eds., *The Columbia History of the World*. New York: Harper & Row, 1972, p. 415.
133. Quoted in Garraty and Gay, *The Columbia History of the World*, p. 415.

Glossary

bailey: A fortified enclosure or space inside the outermost walls of a castle; a courtyard.

benefice: An ecclesiastical office or reward in return for clerical duties; in canon law, a *precarium*.

bestiary: A book describing real or imaginary animals.

book of hours: A prayer book.

bourgeois: A middle-class person.

bourgeoisie: The middle class of a society.

chivalry: The system, spirit, or customs of medieval knighthood.

commune: A usually self-governing settlement organized on the basis of collective ownership and use of goods and property.

courtier: One in attendance at a royal court.

dialectic: Logic; discussion and reasoning by dialogue as a method of intellectual investigation.

fealty: Loyalty; the fidelity of a vassal or feudal tenant to his lord.

feudalism: A method of holding land during the Middle Ages in Europe by giving one's services to the owner.

feudal lord: The master from whom men held land and to whom they owed services under the feudal system.

fief: A feudal estate; something over which one has rights or exercises control.

garderobe: A private room; privy.

hegemony: Dominance of leadership, particularly by one nation over another.

Hellenistic: Of or relating to Greek history, culture, or art after Alexander the Great.

herbary: A book describing medicinal and culinary uses of herbs.

homage: An act done or payment made by a vassal to keep his obligation to his feudal lord.

immunitas: Immunity; the granting of exemptions from taxes or from other impositions due to the central authority.

investiture: The act of establishing in office or ratifying.

keep: The inner stronghold or defensive tower of a castle.

Langobardi: Literally, "Long Beards"; the Lombards, a Germanic tribe that invaded Italy in A.D. 568 and established a kingdom in the Po Valley.

Levant: Name given to the eastern shores of the Mediterranean Sea between western Greece and western Egypt.

liege: A vassal bound to feudal service; a ruler or feudal lord.

linsey-woolsey: A coarse fabric of wool and linen or cotton.

Magyars: The dominant people of Hungary.

motte: An artificial mound or hill serving as a site for a castle.

palisade: A fence of stakes, especially for defense.

paradigm: Something serving as an example or model of how something should be done.

plutocracy: A controlling class of a society composed of the wealthy.

portent: Something that foreshadows a coming event; omen.

psalter: A collection of psalms.

Saracen: An Arab or Muslim at the time of the Crusades.

secular: Concerned with worldly rather than spiritual affairs.

tunic: A hip-length or longer blouse or jacket.

vassal: A person under the protection of a feudal lord to whom he has vowed homage and loyalty; a feudal tenant.

villein: A free peasant.

wattle: A structure of interwoven sticks or twigs, often used as the underlying framework for medieval huts.

Chronology of Events

476
Fall of the Roman Empire.

Early Middle Ages—500 to 900 or 1000

613–987
Reign of Carolingians in western Europe.

768
Charlemagne becomes king of the Franks.

843
Frankish Empire splits into three parts after the death of Charlemagne's son and successor, Louis.

High Middle Ages—900 or 1000 to 1300

969
Church movements introduce the Peace and Truce of God.

1054
Church council in Narbonne expands the terms of the Truce of God, prohibiting Christians from killing fellow Christians.

1066
The Norman Conquest of England led by William the Conqueror.

1085
Pope Gregory VII dies, but the battle of investiture between European sovereigns and the papacy rages on.

1095
Pope Urban II rallies Christian knights and soldiers to defend the Cross in the Holy Land.

1097
First Crusade begins.

1122
Concordat of Worms; compromise reached in investiture conflict.

1161
First *hansa* (commercial association or guild) established at Wisby, on the island of Gotland.

1171
Bank of Venice arranges exchanges of accounts among clients by mere bookkeeping operations.

1235
Cahorsian moneylenders practice usury in England under the guise of trade.

1260–1347
Banking flourishes in Florence.

1284
All major European nations except England now minting gold coinage.

1291
The fall of Acre in the Holy Land marks the end of the eight numbered Crusades.

Late Middle Ages—1300 to 1500

1300
Feudalism effectively ends.

1315–1316
Excessive rains cause crop failures; famine sweeps across Europe.

1320
Wages now decreased by some 25 to 40 percent from a century earlier.

1337–1457
The Hundred Years' War.

1347–1350
The Black Death (bubonic plague pandemic) kills about 25 million people in western and central Europe.

1350
Negotiable credit instruments introduced; mercantile power shifts from the Mediterranean to northwestern Europe.

1350–1453
Epic clash between the Byzantine Empire and the Ottoman Turks.

1381
Peasants' Revolt.

1492
Columbus discovers America.

1500
The Renaissance begins in Europe.

For Further Reading

Timothy Levi Biel, *The Black Death*. San Diego: Lucent Books, 1989. Biel describes how the Black Death shattered the lives of medieval people and ultimately ended the Middle Ages.

———, *The Crusades*. San Diego: Lucent Books, 1995. The author re-creates the series of massive military campaigns that changed the Middle Ages and feudal society.

Bulfinch's Mythology, *The Age of Chivalry and Legends of Charlemagne, or Romance of the Middle Ages*. Garden City, NY: Doubleday, n.d. This thrilling treasury brings the epic sagas and legends of the Middle Ages to life; recalls kings, knights, damsels, and noble quests.

Glyn Burgess, trans., *The Song of Roland*. London: Penguin Books, 1990. The oldest extant epic poem in French; a celebration of the crusading and feudal values of the twelfth century.

James A. Corrick, *The Early Middle Ages*. San Diego: Lucent Books, 1995. Corrick refutes the popular view that the Middle Ages were stagnant and full of superstition.

———, *The Late Middle Ages*. San Diego: Lucent Books, 1995. The author continues his treatise on the Middle Ages, covering the period from 1000 to 1500.

Alfred W. Crosby, *The Measure of Reality: Quantification and Western Society, 1250–1600*. New York: Cambridge University Press, 1997. The author examines how Europeans learned to control their world by breaking reality into equal, arbitrary units.

Eleanor Shipley Duckett, *Death and Life in the Tenth Century*. Ann Arbor: University of Michigan Press, 1991. Duckett depicts, with charm and grace, both the evils and good of the world during one of its least-written-about periods.

Felipe Fernández-Armesto, *Millennium: A History of the Last Thousand Years*. New York: Scribner, 1995. A clear, comprehensive, one-volume history of the world, beginning in 1005 and extending for 990 years.

Amy Kelly, *Eleanor of Aquitaine and the Four Kings*. New York: Book-of-the-Month Club, 1996. Kelly reveals Eleanor's greatness of vision, intelligence, and political sagacity.

John Matthews and Bob Stewart, *Warriors of Christendom: Charlemagne, El Cid, Barbarossa, Richard Lionheart*. Poole, England: Firebird Books, 1988. The story of four great warlords from the early medieval era and how they were influenced by the chivalrous traditions that were beginning to characterize medieval culture.

Don Nardo, *Life on a Medieval Pilgrimage*. San Diego: Lucent Books, 1996. Nardo vividly re-creates the medieval world, focusing on the importance of pilgrimages.

Eileen Power, *Medieval People*. New York: HarperCollins, 1992. The author shows various aspects of medieval social life using such sources as account books, diaries, letters, records, and wills; a classic study of social history.

Bradley Steffens, *The Children's Crusade*. San Diego: Lucent Books, 1991. A tragic tale of a legion of children naive enough to think that they could recapture the Holy City of Jerusalem from the Muslims in 1212 and brave enough to try.

Stephen Turnbull, *The Book of the Medieval Knight*. London: Arms and Armour Press, 1995. Turnbull tells the story of the knight during the fourteenth and fif-teenth centuries—from the victories of Edward III to the fall of Richard III on Bosworth Field.

Ann Wroe, *A Fool and His Money*. New York: Hill and Wang, 1995. The author unravels the mystery of a pot of gold coins found in a drain during the Hundred Years' War.

Thomas A. Brady Jr., Heiko A. Oberman, and James D. Tracy, eds., *Structures and Assertions*. Vol. 1 of *Handbook of European History, 1400–1600: Late Middle Ages, Renaissance, and Reformation*. Grand Rapids, MI: William B. Eerdmans, 1994. A representative selection of current knowledge and thinking on two hundred years of European history.

Ebenezer Cobham Brewer, *Dictionary of Phrase and Fable*, 14th ed. Ed. Ivor H. Evans. New York: Harper & Row, 1989. One of the best-known and best-loved reference books, with an astonishing range of information; a bibliophile's delight.

Norman F. Cantor, *The Civilization of the Middle Ages*. New York: HarperCollins, 1993. The consummate textbook on the Middle Ages for English-speaking peoples.

———, ed., *The Medieval Reader*. New York: HarperCollins, 1994. An intriguing collection of almost a hundred firsthand accounts of the medieval period.

Compton's Interactive Encyclopedia, Version 3.00. Compton's New Media, copyright © 1994, 1995. The CD-ROM version of the venerable encyclopedia.

Madeleine Pelner Cosman, *Medieval Wordbook*. New York: Facts On File, 1996. A volume of interesting etymological and historical facts and explanations of medieval words and phrases.

Joseph Dahmus, *A History of the Middle Ages*. New York: Barnes & Noble Books, 1995. Traces the continuity of the Middle Ages with ancient and modern history, illuminating events and personalities.

Norman Davies, *Europe: A History*. New York: Oxford University Press, 1996. The entire history of Europe in a single volume, written with style, amazing detail, and thoughtful analysis.

R. Ernest Dupuy and Trevor N. Dupuy, *The Encyclopedia of Military History*, rev. ed. New York: Harper & Row, 1977. A complete one-volume reference guide to the world's military history.

Will Durant, *The Age of Faith: A History of Medieval Civilization—Christian, Islamic, and Judaic—from Constantine to Dante: A.D. 325–1300*. Vol. 4 of *The Story of Civilization*. New York: Simon and Schuster, 1950. A masterful survey of the achievements and modern significance of Christian, Islamic, and Judaic life and culture during the Middle Ages.

Einhard and Notker the Stammerer, *Two Lives of Charlemagne*. Trans. Lewis Thorpe. London: Penguin Books, 1969. This volume presents two fascinating, contrasting perceptions of the legendary king of the Franks and first Holy Roman emperor of western Europe.

John Fines, *Who's Who in the Middle Ages*. New York: Barnes & Noble Books, 1995. A biographical dictionary that chronicles the lives of the men and women who dominated the time between the collapse of the Roman Empire and the Renaissance.

David Hackett Fischer, *The Great Wave: Price Revolutions and the Rhythm of History*. New York: Oxford University Press, 1996. Fischer maintains that the first "great wave" of price fluctuations brought an end to the medieval civilization.

John Garraty and Peter Gay, eds., *The Columbia History of the World*. New York:

Harper & Row, 1972. A scholarly narrative history of the world; authoritative and easy to read.

Frances Gies, *The Knight in History*. New York: Harper & Row, 1987. The *Los Angeles Times* lauds this history as "a carefully researched, concise, readable and entertaining account of an institution that remains a part of the Western imagination."

Frances and Joseph Gies, *Cathedral, Forge, and Waterwheel*. New York: HarperCollins, 1994. Credits advances in medieval technology and science for fueling the rapid developments of the Renaissance.

Joseph and Frances Gies, *Life in a Medieval Castle*. New York: Harper & Row, 1974. A well-researched documentary of medieval life as rightfully centered on the castle.

———, *Life in a Medieval City*. New York: Harper & Row, 1969. An excellent account of what is known of life among medieval city dwellers.

John Guy, *Medieval Life*. Tunbridge Wells, England: Addax, 1995. A short, illustrated history of medieval life from 1066 to 1485.

Elizabeth Hallam, ed., *Chronicles of the Age of Chivalry*. London: Tiger Books International, 1995. A comprehensive, illustrated journey through the Plantagenet dynasty from 1216 to 1377.

———, ed., *Chronicles of the Crusades*. Godalming, England: Bramley Books, 1996. Illuminates Muslim civilization as well as the Christian West during the holy wars that dominated the Middle Ages.

———, ed., *The Plantagenet Encyclopedia: An Alphabetical Guide to 400 Years of English History*. New York: Crescent Books, 1996. The remarkable civilization of the medieval world expressed through the lives and times of the Plantagenets.

James Harpur, with Elizabeth Hallam, consultant, *Revelations: The Medieval World*. New York: Henry Holt, 1995. An illustrated volume that reviews the medieval period from a human perspective.

Michael Hicks, *Who's Who in Late Medieval England*. London: Shepheard-Walwyn, 1991. Two hundred short biographies of people from all walks of medieval life, spanning the period 1272–1485.

Nicholas Hooper and Matthew Bennett, *The Cambridge Illustrated Atlas of Warfare: The Middle Ages 768–1487*. Cambridge and New York: Cambridge University Press, 1996. An invaluable companion and guide to the role of warfare throughout the medieval period; excellent coverage of the crusading epic.

Johan Huizinga, *The Autumn of the Middle Ages*. Trans. Rodney J. Payton and Ulrich Mammitzsch. Chicago: University of Chicago Press, 1996. A keen treatise on life, thought, and art in fourteenth- and fifteenth-century France and the Netherlands.

Judy Jones and William Wilson, *An Incomplete Education*. New York: Ballantine Books, 1987. A thousand years of culture brought to the reader with wit, style, and sophistication.

Sherrilyn Kenyon, *The Writer's Guide to Everyday Life in the Middle Ages: The British Isles from 500 to 1500*. Cincinnati: Writer's Digest Books, 1995. Provides a captivating overview of life in northwestern Europe during the Middle Ages.

Julius Kirshner and Karl F. Morrison, eds., *Medieval Europe*. Vol. 4 of *Readings in Western Civilization*. Chicago: University of Chicago Press, 1986. Thoughtful period writings from medieval Europe, illuminating its foundations and developments.

Robert S. Lopez, *The Birth of Europe*. New York: M. Evans, 1967. A reassessment of the Anglo-French view of the Middle Ages by a master historian; well researched and well written.

Bryce D. Lyon, ed., *The High Middle Ages: 1000–1300*. Vol. 5 of *Sources in Western Civilization*, Herbert H. Rowen, gen. ed. New York: Free Press, 1964. A collection of carefully chosen articles depicting the eleventh-century revitalization of Europe.

A. V. B. Norman, *The Medieval Soldier*. New York: Barnes & Noble Books, 1993. Examines the medieval warrior's life, training, weapons and equipment, and rights and obligations under feudalism.

Carole Rawcliffe, *Medicine and Society in Later Medieval England*. Phoenix Mill, England: Alan Sutton, 1995. A highly readable analysis of a fascinating aspect of medieval life.

Jonathan Riley-Smith, *The Crusades: A Short History*. New Haven, CT, and London: Yale University Press, 1987. A behind-the-scenes look at the fierce battles that bloodied the sands of the Holy Land.

Nigel Saul, ed., *Age of Chivalry: Art and Society in Late Medieval England*. London: Brockhampton Press, 1995. Medieval historians explore the nature of the society that produced and patronized the artifacts of the chivalric age.

———, ed., *The Oxford Illustrated History of Medieval England*. New York: Oxford University Press, 1997. A richly illustrated, comprehensive introduction to medieval England.

R. W. Southern, *The Making of the Middle Ages*. New Haven, CT, and London: Yale University Press, 1992. An absorbing study of the main personalities and the influences that shaped western Europe from the late tenth to the early thirteenth century.

Barbara W. Tuchman, *A Distant Mirror: The Calamitous 14th Century*. New York: Ballantine Books, 1979. Tuchman brings history to life in her works, this time energizing life in the fourteenth century by focusing on the life of a French knight.

Christopher Tyerman, *Who's Who in Medieval England*. London: Shepheard-Walwyn, 1996. More than 160 short biographies of men and women who played a prominent role in their time (1066–1272).

Richard Vaughn, trans. and ed., *The Illustrated Chronicles of Matthew Paris: Observations of Thirteenth-Century Life*. Cambridge, England: Alan Sutton, 1993. A unique record of thirteenth-century life, with more than a hundred full-color reproductions of the original manuscript decorations.

Philip Warner, *The Medieval Castle*. New York: Barnes & Noble Books, 1993. A handsomely illustrated volume explaining why and how castles were built and why they dominated medieval life.

Philip Ziegler, *The Black Death*. Phoenix Mill, England: Alan Sutton, 1995. A graphic anecdotal account of the plague that killed about a third of the European population and shattered medieval society.

Index

Round Table, 61, 68

Rules for Monks (St. Benedict), 13

rural life, in Middle Ages, 27–35

    farming, 34–35

    migration to towns, 35

    village life, 32–34

    see also castles, medieval

Sarabites, 13

Saracens (Muslims), 15

scholasticism, defined, 70–71

sciences, of Middle Ages, 72–74

    medicine, 73–74

serfs, 27–28

slavery, 27, 75

social order, in Middle Ages, 16–26

    medieval triangle, 20–26

    see also feudalism

streets, in medieval town, 42

supply-demand inflation, 55

technology and invention, 74–75

Third Estate (middle class), 43

Thomas Aquinas, Saint, 71, 76

towns. *See* urban life

trade

    centers of, 48–50

    routes

        of Hanseatic League, map, 54

        opening of, 37–39

Truce of God, 62

universities, 71–72

University of Paris, 72

Urban II (pope), 37

urban life, 36–46

    city streets, 42

    crime and punishment, 42–44

    middle-class family life, 43–45

    rise of middle class, 37–40

    trade routes and, 37–39

Vandals, 9

vassals, 8–9

    as element of feudalism, 17

Verhansung (commercial boycott), 53

Vikings, 15, 36

    raids, 19, 53

village life, 32–34

war and warriors, 61–64

War of the Roses, 64

William of Ockham, 71

William the Conqueror, 16, 29, 64

witchcraft, 73

Witello (or Vitellon), 73–74

women

    barbarian, 11

    castle life of, 31–32

    clothing of, 21, 33

    middle-class life of, 43, 45

yeomen, as element of middle class, 25–26

Picture Credits

Cover photo: Victoria & Albert Museum, London/Art Resource, NY

Archive Photos, 49, 63

The Book of Kells: Selected Plates in Full Color, ed. Blanche Cirker, Dover Publications, Inc., ©1982, 67

Corbis-Bettmann, 37, 51

Giraudon/Art Resource, NY, 72, 73

Heck's Pictorial Archive of Military Science, Geography and History, ed. J. G. Heck, Dover Publications, Inc., ©1994, 31

Historic Costume in Pictures, Dover Publications, Inc., ©1975, 21, 26, 43

Library of Congress, 14, 35, 44, 58, 65, 74, 79

Medieval Life Illustrations, Carol Belanger Grafton, Dover Publications, Inc., ©1996, 32, 70

North Wind Picture Archives, 9, 16, 18, 20, 23, 28, 34, 41, 48, 77

Picture Book of Devils, Demons and Witchcraft, Ernst and Johanna Lehner, Dover Publications, Inc., ©1971, 57

Scala/Art Resource, NY, 45

Vanni/Art Resource, NY, 66

Weapons and Armor, ed. Harold H. Hart, Dover Publications, Inc., ©1978, 39

About the Author

Earle Rice Jr. attended San Jose City College and Foothill College, on the San Francisco peninsula, after serving nine years with the U.S. Marine Corps.

He has authored more than two dozen books for young adults, including fast-action fiction and adaptations of *Dracula, All Quiet on the Western Front,* and *The Grapes of Wrath.* Mr. Rice has written numerous books for Lucent, including *The Cuban Revolution, The Salem Witch Trials, The Final Solution, Nazi War Criminals, Life During the Crusades,* and seven books in the popular Great Battles series. He has also written articles and short stories, and has previously worked for several years as a technical writer.

Mr. Rice is a former senior design engineer in the aerospace industry who now devotes full-time to his writing. He lives in Julian, California, with his wife, daughter, two granddaughters, four cats, and a dog.